NATURAL TUNNEL
NATURE'S MARVEL IN STONE

TONY SCALES

Note to Readers: Those unfamiliar with Natural Tunnel and its environs would do well to refer to the maps in chapters 6, 9, and 15 as they read the story, which is presented (roughly) chronologically.

ISBN 1-57072-287-0
Copyright © 2004 by Tony Scales
Printed in the United States of America
All Rights Reserved

3 4 5 6 7 8 9 0

For Janice and Stewart, the best life partners a man could ever have. And for my mother, Nellie Virginia, and my brother, Patrick, who passed on before they could see the story told. With loved ones like this to share the path, I wish the journey would never end.

TABLE OF CONTENTS

ACKNOWLEDGMENTS

One day—how long ago now, eight years?—I told Natural Tunnel State Park Manager Craig Seaver I was going to write a book about the Tunnel. I recall that Craig looked at me a little cross-eyed, and I believe I heard him chuckle a little under his breath, but he has been my sounding board and constant supporter since. Thanks, Craig, Craig's family, and all the staff at Natural Tunnel State Park (NTSP), who have shown me and my family nothing but simple kindness and friendship.

I am amazed at the history-discovery process and am now very familiar with the Law of Diminishing Returns, finding that sometimes weeks of searching result in a single-line entry, or nothing at all. Every lead would require that I call on someone for help and guidance. Invariably, those I would ask would share their time and knowledge and shorten my learning curve. At risk of leaving someone out, and in no particular order, they are: Dr. Craig Ashbrook, Southwest Virginia Community College; Dr. Michael C. Clark, University of Tennessee; Dr. Tony Waltham, Nottingham Technological University; Dr. John Holsinger, Old Dominion University; Bill Balfour, Lynn D. Haynes, and Gary L. Egan, Certified Professional Geologists; Bill Cawood, former NTSP chief ranger and the best woodsman I know; Dave Hubbard, Virginia Division of Mineral Resources; Stewart Adam Scales, NTSP volunteer par excellence and a son who makes the word *proud* seem meager.

Kevin Castle of the *Kingsport Times-News* wrote an article on my project for his paper, which opened many doors. Through interest in that piece, I had the pleasure to meet or converse with a number of local residents with stories to tell and ties to the Tunnel, including Sylvia Bowling Tompkins, Ottalee Winegar, J. M. Fraley, Jewel Willis, Kyle and Mildred Jenkins, Rosalee (Jenkins) Gross, Ruby Stewart, Shirley Adair (who shared the letter from her distant cousin, describing the Schaffer/Lane elopement), Ron Walker, Jimmy Frazier, and Maggie (Wells/Maggard) Lawson.

Thanks are also due to the following people, simply by doing their job or going out of their way to help: the Honorable Ford C. Quillen, Jack Quillen, Ron Flanary, John Dale (who freely shared his collection of Southern Railway's Appalachia Division guides and timetables), the University of Virginia College at Wise John Cook Wyllie Library (particularly librarians Amelia VanGundy and Kim Marshall), the Scott County Public Library, the C. Bascom Slemp Memorial Library, Ted Polk (interlibrary loan librarian at the Library of Virginia), Stuart and Delores Miller, Richard Whitt, Gil Bledsoe (former NTSP Manager), Janet Blevins (former NTSP manager) and Sharon Ewing of the Southwest Virginia Museum, Maynard Hawkins (a descendant of Uncle Ike who traced that story for me), Bill Hendrick, Ken Murray, and Leslie Bright (my "rock caddy").

To present and former NTSP and Virginia Department of Conservation and Recreation staff and volunteers Robert Chapman, Doug Smith, Nancy Horton, Nancy Bledsoe, Mildred Esteppe, Mildred Sturgill, Lisa Bishop, Saundra Tomlinson, Ishmael Richardson, Woody Dillon, Ron Trask, Arthur Cope, Rosa Chambers, Jodie Kern, Ginger Kern, Sharon Mize, Kevin Kelly, Jill Grizzle, Bob VanGundy, Gary Cody, Marty McConnell, Gladys Allen, Dawn Shank, Nancy Heltman, Holly Walker, and Jean Brown, thanks from "Stewart's dad."

The first draft of this book was reviewed by Michael D. Abbott, Craig Ashbrook, Bill Balfour, Bill Cawood, Gary Egan, Bob Harvey, Lynn Haynes, Stan Johnson, Stuart Miller, and Craig Seaver. Any improvements resulting I owe to these gentlemen; any errors are mine and mine alone. And I should be quick to point out that opinions and conclusions herein are mine, and by no means reflect upon these good people or their institutions.

How do you make a dream come true? All would be for naught if not for my publisher, The Overmountain Press, a treasure for all "Franklinians" and preservers and recorders of this fair land. More than a publisher of books, they are a family, a family who loves place, a family who loves time, a family who loves the written word. Beth Wright, Daniel Lewis, Heather Richardson, Angela Mann, and Penny Street, at the very least for putting up with me—thank you. To my editor, Jason Weems, whose attention to detail not only made this book better but also made it shine, I simply say this—may the water under your hull always be white.

The most special thanks are due two gentlemen whose love for history and railroading are legendary and whose different approaches are boons to a would-be researcher. Robert L. Harvey is a warehouse of knowledge on East Tennessee and Southwest Virginia railroading and other subjects of equal import, and he freely shared his materials and insights with me—even to the point of transcribing documents and old newspaper articles—with no other driving force than his love of the subject. He contacted me through the *Kingsport Times-News* article and accepted me as a bona fide writer/researcher when all I had was an idea. Getting the railroad story right—and boy, Bob, I hope I did, or I'll never hear the end of it—is due to him.

Where Bob is the railroad philosopher, Kenny Fannon is the railroad pack rat, and I spent many an enjoyable—and dusty—day rummaging through his enormous collection of railroad memorabilia. When I would find something of interest, he'd say "take it," with no more directive than "bring it back when you're done." If you're ever through Duffield, you must stop by Kenny's. You can't miss his place—it's the railroad depot and caboose at the stoplight.

There are two times I would like to have visited the Tunnel in the past. One would be with Lieutenant Colonel Long, looking upon that great cavern with no railroad in sight or even thought of, when he fired his musket to produce "a crash-like report." The other would be when the SA&O passed through the first time—and I would like to have Kenny at the throttle and Bob on the bell.

FOREWORD

The goal of presenting a history of Natural Tunnel has been achieved. The author contributes much to the recognition of the importance of Natural Tunnel and its place in the history of Southwest Virginia. It is a major contribution that brings hundreds of items of information from courthouses, public and private records, and from personal communications with local citizens into one source. These items relate to "tales and facts" that the author has woven into an easily readable book. This book is a much-needed contribution for the general public to have an understanding of the history of Natural Tunnel, from its geologic beginning to its present status as a state park.

The book is important at this time because as development continues, we need to pay due regard to our natural environment and in this case the geologic history and conditions that created this great natural feature. Natural Tunnel is one of the great natural sites formed directly by geologic processes of weathering, erosion, and solution acting slowly over thousands of years.

The recent geologic research that gives us an understanding of the events that resulted in the Tunnel's creation has greatly advanced our knowledge. The author's presentation has resulted in an orderly history of the "ups and downs" of the "life" of Natural Tunnel.

Stanley S. Johnson
State Geologist of Virginia, 1992-2002

INTRODUCTION

I remember the first time I visited the Natural Tunnel of Scott County, a neighboring county of my home in Cleveland, Virginia. I was awestruck with this immense exposure of limestone cliffs, caves, and deep gorges, just as most are when they first train their eyes on the gaping chasm, which extends hundreds of feet downward and into the Tunnel. Breathtaking! I had to learn all I could about this natural feature. To understand the Tunnel, I tried to unearth as much information about this geologically haunting structure as I could. That information-gathering episode sought references that could explain the facts and culture surrounding the Tunnel's geologic development and history. My journey revealed many sources, but too few to complete the picture. Some were no longer available, and others fragmentary. I found no individual source containing all the answers to my numerous questions—until now.

The author offers the only comprehensive account of Natural Tunnel's geologic development and cultural history. The reader will find no better compilation of well-documented and meticulously assembled explanations of the Tunnel's development, written for both scientists and nonscientists alike. The history of the tunnel, as offered by the author, is clearly presented and covers a multitude of uses spanning the cultural years of one of Mother Nature's most amazing features. The railroad history of the Tunnel is as fascinating as its geology. Railroad buffs will love the stories, the historical photographs, and the captivating documentation of a past era.

I read few books that leave me so captured that I must continue until I reach the final chapter. The author's writings and collection of historical photographs are unsurpassed. His chronology of the Tunnel's bygone days is as complete as I have encountered. Tony Scales's ability to explain complex geology in an understandable way is equally extraordinary. Anyone with a smattering of interest in local history or geology will benefit from his undertaking. This book is an absolute necessity for scientists, local and regional historians, geographers, educators, environmental scientists, and laypeople from all walks of life, whether they have experienced the Tunnel or not.

In a word: unrivaled!

Dr. Craig M. Ashbrook, RPG, REM
Professor of Environmental Management
Southwest Virginia Community College

PROLOGUE

I have been fortunate to become Natural Tunnel State Park's "pet geologist"—whether by merit or default, I don't know—and have been involved with the park and its programs as a volunteer since 1981. Natural Tunnel State Park, and for that matter many of our nation's parks, is centered on a geologic wonder. You do not need to be a geologist or botanist or historian to recognize that Natural Tunnel is unique, even awe-inspiring. I take great pleasure in leading field trips to the park, and one of my favorite ploys is to take first-time visitors down the Tunnel Trail without letting them view the Tunnel from the overlook. This way, their introduction to the reason for the park hits them squarely in the face. Invariably, the jaw drops, followed by "Wow!" and then, "I wonder how it formed. . . ."

The essence of the park is geology, and the essence of this book is not to do away with the wonder but to shed a little light on the geologic reasons for the sights to be found here. In the end, I hope these words will help you grow in your appreciation for this wonderful place.

When I first thought of writing this book, the simple premise was a guidebook, written for the layman from the geologist's perspective. Geologists are the ultimate historians, purveyors of explanations of how a landscape came to be. This role is tempered by the concept of "deep time," the seeing back into ages when obviously no man existed. But as I traveled down this trail, gathering information for this mostly scientific task, a number of side trails appealed to me, trails based on some of the most basic questions we have about time and place. Who was the first to see this? Who was the first to write about it, to describe it? How did people view this wonder? As a treasure or a resource to be exploited? Who owned it, and why would anybody own a "hole through the mountain?"

So I followed these trails. Some were clear and wide, with an obvious beginning and a satisfying conclusion. But many had no clear beginning, were strewn with obstacles in the path, and some just withered to scufflings in the leaves. Then I would retrace my steps, not entirely sure of where I had been but a little more knowledgeable of the place and time, walking where others had been before, and blazing just a few new leads myself. As wiser men have noted, the joy is not in the arrival, but in the journey.

Come on, let's go for a walk. Wear your hiking boots.

Tony Scales
Big Stone Gap, Virginia

DISCOVERY AND THE WORD GETS OUT

THE FIRST DESCRIPTIONS OF NATURAL TUNNEL, 1750-1832

THERE IS, OVER STOCK CREEK, A BRANCH OF CLINCH RIVER, A BRIDGE, WHOSE HEIGHT IS ESTIMATED AT 300 FEET, WITH A THICKER ARCH; WHOSE FORMATION, IN EVERY MATERIAL RESPECT, RESEMBLES THAT OF ITS MORE CELEBRATED RIVAL OF ROCKBRIDGE.

—FRANCIS WALKER GILMER, 1816

DURING THE PAST SUMMER, I VISITED A REMARKABLE NATURAL BRIDGE IN SCOTT COUNTY, VIRGINIA, TO WHICH I HAVE GIVEN THE NAME OF NATURAL TUNNEL, ON ACCOUNT OF ITS STRIKING RESEMBLANCE TO ARTIFICIAL STRUCTURES OF THAT KIND.

—LIEUTENANT COLONEL STEPHEN H. LONG, 1832

egend has it—which is actually a polite way to say, "it would be nice to believe"—that the first non-Native American to see Natural Tunnel was the renowned explorer Daniel Boone. Though Boone left no record of the Tunnel, a bit of logical reasoning leads to the belief that he did see it. The famed Wilderness Road blazed by Boone passes through Tunnel Gap in Purchase Ridge at the present entrance to Natural Tunnel State Park (NTSP), a mere 1000 feet from the point where Stock Creek emerges from the South Portal of Natural Tunnel. Note that Tunnel Gap is not a gap separating two different creek drainages—leave Stock Creek on either side of the gap, cross over, descend, and you're back on Stock Creek.

Boone, as all explorers, would have followed the easiest route of travel, that is, natural drainages. But in ascending Stock Creek from its confluence with the Clinch River, upon approaching the Tunnel, he would find himself in a narrow gorge—the "chasm" to be discussed later in this book—with near-vertical walls on either side, not a pleasant setting for a backwoodsman in Indian territory. And then, after rounding a bend in the creek, he would find himself facing an awesome sight—a horseshoe of cliffs (the Amphitheater) towering upwards of 400 feet, a sheer rock wall. Again, not a good place for the long hunter.

At the southern entrance of the Tunnel, where Stock Creek spills into the Amphitheater (assuming he would choose to fight his way through deadwood and brush piled up by high water), Boone would peer into a huge maw, floored by the stream, great rock boulders, and more deadwood—not the best of footpaths. He would see no light ahead, for Stock Creek makes an S curve traversing the Tunnel, and it is impossible to see from one opening to the other. Searching for a path of least resistance, and likely thinking it a cave, he would determine that a better way had to be found, retrace his steps, and then discover the ephemeral drainage leading to Tunnel Gap, cross the gap and descend, and once again find Stock Creek where it flows into the North Portal.

Even recognizing it as the same creek, Boone would still not know it flowed through a tunnel, unable to see from one end to the other. No stranger to caves and overhangs as shelters, it seems likely he would have filed the "cave" away in his memory for future need. However, there is no record that he told anyone of his find, if indeed he did visit the site.

Such would be the story of Natural Tunnel for over 100 years after Boone's assumed "discovery." As the old saying goes, "you can't get there from here," and in the 19th century, a journey to see Natural Tunnel was not a casual affair nor an afternoon lark. But when word of this great natural wonder got out, scientists, tourists, and adventurers determined that viewing the sight was worth the trouble, and they solved the problem of not being able to "get there from here"—they started from somewhere else!

Lying just a short walk from the Wilderness Road, it is reasonable to assume at least some of the myriad of travelers to the Kentucky bluegrass and points west would have visited the Tunnel and left some record of it, say, in a letter or journal. In his *History of Scott County Virginia*, Robert M. Addington notes that most travelers in the late 1700s who left record of their journeys invariably men-

tioned Little Flat Lick—the site of present Duffield, Virginia, just northwest of Natural Tunnel—but, "On the other hand, not one has deemed it worth while to make mention of the Great Natural Tunnel, which lay directly across his path traveling through Stock Creek Valley." Addington is incorrect that the Tunnel lay "directly" across the traveler's way, and while a detour along Stock Creek from the Wilderness Road would be a difficult path, a walker would take but five minutes to get to the nearest overlook from Tunnel Gap, even through dense woods.

Many a traveler would have passed by, and even over, the Tunnel. Besides the Wilderness Road going through Tunnel Gap, the old Fincastle Road, coming west from Rye Cove, passes near the North Portal. Today, as you drive Route 650 through the park, your wheels roll over the footprints of these pioneers. And certainly during the opening of these routes to the north and west, settlers and forts, notably Rye Cove and Carters forts only a short distance away, were present in the area, with even the revered Boone residing for a while in neighboring Castlewood and hunting in the area. It seems as though many would have seen, but no one wrote.

So how did word of Natural Tunnel get out? As in many aspects of life in the early 19th century, with a restless nation of marginally literate people on the move, and the country expanding westward, word of something "new" would pass from person to person until someone would take it on himself to verify what he'd been told. Word of Natural Tunnel made its way to mapmakers, and by 1814, Natural Tunnel had entered the American lexicon and was shown on Mathew Carey's map of Virginia (see Figure 1). On this map, Natural Tunnel is denoted as "Natural Bridge," a generic term for any archlike rock for-

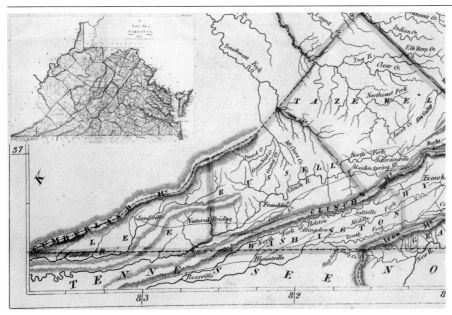

Figure 1. Mathew Carey's 1814 map of Virginia (inset) and an enlargement of the far southwestern portion of that map. Note that Natural Tunnel is designated as "Natural Bridge" and lies on the Lee/Russell county border (present Scott County was formed from parts of Lee, Russell, and Washington counties in November of 1814). (From the David Rumsey Historical Map Collection)

Bridge reads well even by today's understanding of geology, and he correctly intuited the roles of soluble rocks, drainage, and erosion. To support his theory, he pointed to Natural Bridge's marked similarity to Natural Tunnel (though not yet known by that name), thus beginning a theme that has haunted Natural Tunnel to this day, comparing the smaller but more accessible Natural Bridge to its larger but remote "country cousin." Reading Gilmer's paper, it is not clear if he actually visited Natural Tunnel, but he was the grandson of legendary Southwest Virginia explorer Dr. Thomas Walker, so we may assume his knowledge was more than passing.

But for the Tunnel to become more than a point on the map, it needed the right exposure. Fortunately for Americans, and for the legacy of the Tunnel, the first man to visit and record his observations was Lieutenant Colonel Stephen H. Long, a scientist and keen observer.

Before his visit to the Tunnel, Long (see Figure 3) had risen to prominence in the United States Army Corps of Topographical Engineers. In 1817, he explored the Upper Mississippi River and helped establish Fort Smith, Arkansas. In 1820, he explored the Platte, Red, and Arkansas rivers. In 1823, he explored the sources of the Minnesota and Red rivers and established the United States/Canada boundary west of the Great Lakes.

Following these adventures, Long was assigned by the War Department as a consulting engineer to the Baltimore and Ohio Railroad, and he is impor-

mation spanning a valley (there are many natural bridges across North America), not to be confused with the Natural Bridge discussed below.

The first written account of Natural Tunnel appeared in 1816, when Francis Walker Gilmer (see Figure 2), a protégé of Thomas Jefferson who, among other duties, assisted Jefferson by recruiting staff for the new University of Virginia in Charlottesville, presented a paper to the American Philosophical Society in Philadelphia. Gilmer discussed the formation of the famous Natural Bridge—owned by Jefferson—of Rockbridge County, Virginia, challenging the great man himself by refuting Jefferson's theory of formation by "some sudden and violent convulsion of nature."

Gilmer's theory of the formation of Natural

Figure 2. Francis Walker Gilmer, 1790-1826. Gilmer, a protégé of Thomas Jefferson, presented the first known written account of Natural Tunnel in 1816 to the American Philosophical Society, comparing its formation to that of Natural Bridge in Rockbridge County, Virginia. It is not known if Gilmer, the grandson of famous explorer Dr. Thomas Walker, actually visited Natural Tunnel. Courtesy of Historical Collections & Services, Claude Moore Health Sciences Library, University of Virginia. (Portrait by unknown artist, circa 1820)

tant to the history of railroading as the author of the 1829 *Rail Road Manual*. Subsequently, he surveyed railroad routes in Georgia and Tennessee, and he continued his consulting career with the railroad industry until his death in Illinois, near the end of the Civil War, where he was overseeing navigation improvements on the Mississippi River.

It is fitting, if not curiously coincidental, that a man of importance to railroading should be the first to describe the Tunnel, which in later years would serve as a natural route for the South Atlantic and Ohio Railroad, later the Virginia & Southwestern, then Southern, then Norfolk Southern.

But at the time of his visit, in the summer of 1831, Long was not scouting railroad routes but rather a wagon road from Linville, North Carolina, to Pikeville, Kentucky, under a directive of President Andrew Jackson to the United States Topographical Bureau. Likely Long was also consulting on railroad design in the area, and the use of the Tunnel as a passage for a rail line probably passed his mind, though the Tunnel is not even mentioned in his final report. His task was to define a route for foot and beast, and little was known at that time of the economic riches—coal—that would drive the construction of railroads in Southwest Virginia at the end of the century.

Regardless, Lieutenant Colonel Long reported his observations in an article entitled "Description of a Natural Tunnel, in Scott County, Virginia" published in the March 1832 *Monthly American Journal of Geology and Natural Science* (interestingly, this issue also contains a letter by a young naturalist named John James Audubon, reporting on his travels in Florida). In his first sentence, Long states, "I visited a remarkable natural bridge . . . ," but he then corrects and clarifies his description, stating, "to which I have given the name of Natural tunnel, on account of its striking resemblance to artificial structures of that kind." Thus Long not only became the first to provide a direct written description of the Tunnel, he provided the name as well.

Long's somewhat flowery language and run-on sentences, common at that time, came to be plagia-

Figure 3. Lieutenant Colonel Stephen H. Long, 1784-1864. Renowned western explorer Long, with the United States Army Corps of Topographical Engineers, visited Natural Tunnel in 1831 while surveying a wagon road from Linville, North Carolina, to Pikeville, Kentucky. His 1832 report, the first published firsthand description of Natural Tunnel, served to firmly set this wonder before the American people. (From the collections of Independence National Historical Park. Artist Titian Peale, circa 1820)

rized by later authors—many of whom had never visited the Tunnel! But his descriptions, if the man-made changes are removed in the mind's eye, are just as applicable today as in 1831. Further, we are fortunate to have an engraving made at that time showing the South Portal (see Figure 4). Though rendered with a bit of artistic license, it does capture the grandeur of the South Portal and the Amphi-

theater and would have sparked the interest of the readers to have a personal look.

The word was out—the far reaches of Virginia held a sight worth seeing. Interestingly, even at this early date, word had spread "across the pond." Soon after Long's work was published, no doubt a fast packet boat delivered that article to the docks of London, where the periodical *The Mirror of Literature, Amusement, and Instruction* saw in it interest to their readers and reprinted a shortened version, accompanied by an altered version of the Childs and Inman engraving (see Figure 5).

SIDE TRAIL

Lieutenant Colonel Long's description of the Tunnel is remarkably detailed. While not quite as thorough, the final paragraph, summarizing the general character of the region around the Tunnel, is succinct and encompasses all those geologic traits that would make the highlands of Virginia, Tennessee, Kentucky, North Carolina, and (later) West Virginia the object of future exploration and exploitation:

"The rocks found in this part of the country are principally sandstone and limestone, in stratifications nearly horizontal, with occasional beds of clay slate. A mixture of the two former frequently occurs among the alternations presented by these rocks. A variety of rock resembling the French burr, occurs in abundance on Butcher's fork, of Powell's river, about twenty miles northwardly of the natural tunnel. Fossils are more or less abundant in these and other rocks. Fossil bones of an interesting character have been found in several places. Saltpetre caves are numerous. Coves, sinks, and subterranean caverns are strikingly characteristic, not only of the country circumjacent to the natural tunnel, but of the region generally situated between the Cumberland mountain and the Blue ridge or Apalachian [sic] mountain. Bituminous coal, with its usual accompaniments, abounds in the northerly parts of this region; and in the intermediate and southerly portions; iron, variously combined, often magnetic, together with talcose rocks, &c. &c, are to be met with in great abundance."

Figure 4. This Childs and Inman wood engraving accompanies Lieutenant Colonel Long's 1832 article on Natural Tunnel in *The Monthly American Journal of Geology and Natural Science.* The artist who supplied the sketch, identified by Long only as "a particular friend in this city," has tried to put into the view portions of the Amphitheater, described by Long as a "mural precipice," that can not be seen in a single view. Further, Stock Creek does not actually fill the valley bottom as shown, and the steep slope below Shelter Caves is not shown.

Figure 5. This engraving, altered from the one that accompanies Long's original article, appeared in the December 29, 1832, issue of *The Mirror of Literature, Amusement, and Instruction,* a London periodical. Note that the gentleman in the foreground, who previously was just admiring the view, is now fishing for his supper.

YOU CAN'T GET THERE FROM HERE
NATURAL TUNNEL IN LITERATURE, 1832-1890

BUT SUCH AS IT IS, OR AS I HAVE HEARD IT DESCRIBED BY AN INTELLIGENT VISITOR (FOR I HAVE NOT SEEN IT), YOU WILL READILY CONCEIVE THAT IT IS A RARE AND INTERESTING CURIOSITY, AND ONE THAT WOULD BE MUCH VISITED, IF "DAME NATURE" HAD NOT (AS IF JEALOUS OF SHOWING TOO MANY OF HER WORKS OF INTERNAL IMPROVEMENT) HIDDEN IT AMONG RUGGED MOUNTAINS, IN A PLACE REMOTE FROM THE GREAT HIGHWAYS OF TRAVEL.

—THE REVEREND H. RUFFNER, 1839

he word was out by the early 1800s. There was a natural wonder in Southwest Virginia worth the time and trouble to see. But how could you get there?

Before 1856, when the Virginia & Tennessee Railroad (V&T) was completed to Bristol, Tennessee/Virginia, the trek to Natural Tunnel was an adventure in backwoods and muddy paths. Thus, the first visitors to the Tunnel were usually locals, that is, tourists from points in Virginia and Tennessee east and south of the Tunnel. The nearest "large" settlement to the Tunnel was Estillville, now Gate City, which served as the staging area for travelers to the Tunnel. Later, the railroad would allow visitors from a wider area to journey there, but all would have to make their way to Estillville for the "jump-off." Many report leaving that town, traveling to the Tunnel by wagon or horseback, and staying with local folk, who not only housed and fed them but also served as guides. Thus, even in the early 19th century, Southwest Virginians were dabbling in the tourist trade.

While rigors of such travel were quietly accepted at that time, even hardy travelers who recorded their journeys couldn't help but mention that a trip to the Tunnel was a bit grueling. This difficulty was due to the setting of the Tunnel itself. It pierces Purchase Ridge, a typical Southwest Virginia ridge in that it's "steeper than a cow's face." If the traveler chose to access the Tunnel from the North Portal, he had to negotiate Purchase Ridge. If he chose to visit via the South Portal, he had to "run the chasm," the gorge of Stock Creek, with sheer slopes and even vertical cliffs in places. And both approaches would have been lined with rock fall and flood debris, the latter primarily trees washed down Stock Creek or toppled into the chasm from atop Purchase Ridge. At that time, many of these would have been enormous trees of the as-yet-uncut Appalachian chestnut/oak forest.

An early visitor, known only by the initials "W. H. C.," reported his observations in an 1844 issue of *The Southern Literary Messenger*, touching on many of the stories and themes—real or imagined—that can be traced throughout the Tunnel's recorded history. Importantly, he noted the presence of saltpeter (an essential ingredient in gunpowder) workings at the tunnel. He also introduced, for the first time, "a tradition current in the neighborhood"—meaning told to him by locals—the story of an intrepid saltpeter prospector named Dotson hanging perilously from the sheer walls of the Amphitheater. Later, this story would appear again and again, twisted and embellished through time.

W. H. C. could not help, as most visitors did, comparing the Tunnel to Natural Bridge, but credit is due him in that he is the first to state the superior size and form of the Tunnel, noting, "Born in the neighborhood of the Natural Bridge, I had been taught to consider it the master work of Nature: but this prejudice to the contrary notwithstanding, I know not if the bridge can claim the palm from its rival of the South-West."

Lastly, he decried the lack of public awareness of this wonder, attributing this lack to the Tunnel's backwoods setting in rugged country, though he states that this remoteness was no longer a consideration because, "A capital road has been lately constructed, passing within less than a mile of the spot; and I understand that the people of the neighborhood are about to make a passable road down the creek immediately to the arch." What "capital" road he refers to is unknown; until the coming of the railroad, most visitors continued to complain of the difficulty of passage, and, indeed, until passage eased, the Tunnel was visited by few.

As early as 1852, only 23 years after the locomotive "Tom Thumb" lost its race with a horse, and the "Best Friend of Charleston" chugged out of its namesake, somebody was looking at making the muddy paths into iron rails. That somebody was the Virginia & Tennessee Railroad. By way of a branch line, the V&T hoped to gain access to the rich mineral lands of the Appalachian Mountains.

In 1852 (or possibly as early as 1849), Chief Engineer Charles F. M. Garnett was in charge of a survey from Abingdon to the Cumberland Gap. The map from that survey (see Figure 6) shows that, even then, the route was obvious. The Tunnel afforded an easy path through Purchase Ridge. But that idea would have to wait. The V&T never followed through on their plans, and the Civil War delayed development for many years. Until 1890, a trip to the Tunnel took place on foot or beast.

Most early 19th-century literary accounts of the Tunnel are suspiciously repetitive, if not plagiaristic. Certainly, visitation of the Tunnel continued, but little original thought or description can be found. In 1845, Henry Howe published *Historical Collections of Virginia*. The entry on Scott County consists primarily of a description of the Tunnel, quoting at length Long's paper and retelling the story of Poor Dotson. A wood engraving looking out the South Portal was included (see Figure 7).

Many travelogue publications of the day, describing the scenery of the growing nation, deemed a passing reference to the Tunnel requisite when discussing Virginia. For example, in 1850, *The Southern Quarterly Review*, published in Columbia, South Carolina, while extolling the must-sees of Virginia, listed "the natural tunnel of Scott County."

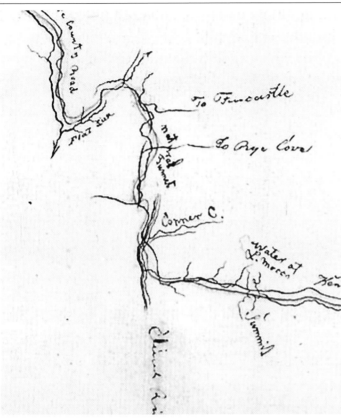

Figure 6. A portion of the circa-1852 map showing the proposed route of a railroad line from Abingdon, Virginia, to the Cumberland Gap, passing through Natural Tunnel. Virginia & Tennessee Railroad Chief Engineer Charles F. M. Garnett caused a survey to be made for a branch line to be called the Virginia and Kentucky. (From the Library of Virginia)

Interestingly, the *Debow's Review*, published in New Orleans, Louisiana, in March of the following year, contains the same wording. *The Southern Democratic Review* published an article that year entitled "Land of the Cherokee," and the writer, apparently pleading lack of time and energy, regrets he could not wax poetic on the Natural Tunnel in Scott County, though he does describe "the faint outlines of the misty, snow-clad summits of Mount Mitchel [sic] and Black Mountain, the highest peaks in the United States."

Also in 1851, Howe published his *Historical Collections of the Great West*. The short article entitled "The Natural Tunnel" is little more than a distillation of Long's description (with no credit assigned) of the Tunnel. Included was another wood engraving looking out of the South Portal but differing from the 1845 book (see Figure 8). Of course, the saltpeter-hunter/human-pendulum story was retold.

Mention of the Tunnel was also required in gazetteers and encyclopedias of the day, and they, too, copied from each other and seldom, if ever, ground-truthed the nature and size of the Tunnel. Some mentioned only the height (most were correct in stating 70-80 feet) of the Tunnel itself but ignored the most prominent visual feature, the Amphitheater cliffs. The height of these, when reported, varied from 100 feet (much too low), to 300 feet (about right), to 500 feet (much too high). Stock Creek was invariably mentioned, but Johnson's 1875 *New Universal Cyclopaedia* put the Tunnel in Clinch Mountain, with the Clinch River running through it! Perhaps we can forgive Mr. Johnson when we consider that James Dabney McCabe, in *The Great Republic* of 1871, showed a woodcut (the same as in Pollard's book, see below) of the Tunnel, labeled as "Natural Bridge"!

One of the most enjoyable and original selections from this period before the railroad, the "era of the intrepid tourist," is in *Harper's New Monthly Magazine* of October 1857. A fanciful article entitled "A Winter in the South" describes the travels of the Broadacre family and friends, on a lark through the Southland. Though written almost as a novella, it is apparent that the author actually visited the locale and turned the tale to appeal to a wider range of readers. The article includes a number of woodcut views by David Hunter Strother (who wrote and

THE NATURAL TUNNEL.

The Natural Tunnel is in the southwestern part of Virginia, three hundred and fifty-six miles from Richmond, near the line of Tennessee. This passage through a mountain is about four hundred and fifty feet in length. A stream of water passes through it and a stage road over it. The above is an internal view, taken near the lower entrance, looking out upon the wall of rock beyond, shown on page 466. At the point where the figures are seen, the roof is estimated at about ninety feet above the stream, and the strata is there arranged in concentric circles, bearing a striking resemblance to a dome.

THE NATURAL TUNNEL.

"To give an adequate idea of this remarkable curiosity, the reader has but to imagine a creek passing through a deep, narrow rock-bound valley, encountering, in its course, a mountain of some 300 feet in height, and winding through it by a huge subterranean cavern."

Figure 7. This engraving comes from Henry Howe's 1845 *Historical Collections of Virginia*. Note the gentleman in the foreground apparently in buckskin and coonskin cap.

illustrated many articles for the magazine and published under the name "Porte Crayon") that reasonably reflect the Tunnel and environs.

From the newly laid V&T Railroad at Bristol, the Broadacre party departed for Knoxville because "at present there is an unfinished gap of seventy miles,

Figure 8. This wood engraving is from Henry Howe's 1851 *Historical Collections of the Great West*. The view is looking out of the South Portal. Stock Creek is shown filling the Tunnel, which it never has except in flood. This and the 1845 engraving more correctly portray the size and height of the interior of the Tunnel than later ones.

over which the traveler is carried in old-fashioned stage-coaches." Apparently the author was a man of the modern age! At Blountville they hired a cart and driver for the trip to Natural Tunnel. They intended to spend the night at Estillville, but "the sight of a wretched, unwashed village, and three taverns vying with each other in dirt and lonesomeness, quite appalled the ladies," so they traveled on to Clinchport for the night.

The next morning, they approached the Tunnel via the present park entrance, viewed the Amphitheater from the present Tunnel Overlook (Eagles Nest), passed around the top of the South Portal, visited Lover's Leap (almost losing a young child to a fall over the cliff), traveled over Tunnel Hill, and descended to the North Portal for a walk-through. Many of the woodcuts included are surprisingly realistic (see Figures 9 and 10), though some are exaggerated (see Figures 11, 12, and 13), perhaps because of the artist's desire to fit in one view objects that cannot actually be seen together. And of course, the author must tell us of Poor Dotson.

Also in 1857, the book *Adventures of Hunters and Travellers, and Narratives of Border Warfare*, authored by "An Old Hunter," appeared. What would now be called a knock-off, this strange collection of tales offered no new information on the Tunnel, and even strangely proclaimed the roof of the Tunnel to be 900 feet high, while putting the Amphitheater walls at 300 feet. An accompanying engraving is almost laughable and gives the reader the impression that one can see completely through the Tunnel (see Figure 14).

In 1870, *The Hamilton Literary Monthly* published Robert L. Bachman's "The Natural Bridge." Mr. Bachman, indeed, took the literary approach to his discourse on the Tunnel, and while he describes it with some accuracy, he can not help but wander into rapture, including, "There, in all the grandeur and solemnity of this place, the naturalist, with the Patriarch of old, might well and reverently exclaim, 'Jehovah-jireh.'"

Probably the most enjoyable account of the Tunnel from this time is found in Edward Pollard's *The Virginia Tourist,* published in 1871. He devotes a chapter to "A Week in South-West Virginia." Like the Broadacres, Pollard arrived by train in Bristol and found little changed, noting the dependence on wagon and horse travel in the neighborhood, "that curious and primitive apparition of commerce [wagon-trade] which we remember in our boyhood in other parts of Virginia, and which we supposed had disappeared since the advent of the steam-car." Another modern man!

Opting for a horseback trip, Pollard followed the same route as the Broadacres and found Estillville, again, lacking. Thirsty after his long ride, he lamented the fact that Scott was a dry county, but he spent the night there and then continued on to the Tunnel.

In his book, Mr. Pollard describes in good detail the Tunnel and its environs, but like Bachman, he, too, was emotionally moved, particularly from walking the Tunnel, passing from the darkness into the light, where "we cast off the confinements of the black space through which we have passed, and we are instantly introduced to a scene so luminous and majestic that in a moment our trembling eyes are captivated and our hearts lifted in unutterable worship of the Creator's work." It would seem the 19th-century man could not visit the Tunnel without having a religious experience!

Included with the chapter are two engravings by Van Ingen and Snyder (see Figures 15 and 16), the latter also found in McCabe's book, though mislabeled. Of course, Mr. Pollard must tell us the story of saltpeter-collecting Dotson (though he spells it

Figures 9, 10, 11, 12, and 13. This series of engravings was included in the October 1857 *Harper's New Monthly Magazine*. The first two, looking out of the South Portal and down from Lover's Leap, are fairly realistic views. The view looking into the South Portal has Stock Creek at about the right size, but the entrance is actually much taller. The interior view shows a series of arches that are not present, and the view of Lover's Leap places it south of the Eagles Nest, whereas it is east.

NATURAL TUNNEL.

Figure 14. This engraving accompanies a short chapter in the book *Adventures of Hunters and Travellers, and Narratives of Border Warfare* and certainly shows that the artist never visited the Tunnel. (Courtesy of Ellen Palmer)

THE NATURAL TUNNEL—THE INTERIOR.

Figure 15. This engraving by Van Ingen and Snyder is from Edward Pollard's *The Virginia Tourist*, 1871. This apparently shows a view out of the North Portal, though the roof is by no means this high.

"Dodson"), but importantly, he devotes a section of the chapter to a description of a visit to Bowlin Cave, often a side trip for visitors to the Tunnel.

In 1874, the book *Picturesque America,* taken from a series of 20 separate monthly printings available by subscription, was published, ostensibly under the auspices and editorship of William Cullen Bryant. Bryant was the first American poet to achieve some international acclaim, and it appears likely that his name was attached to this book, composed mostly of engravings of American scenes, as a marketing ploy. While offering no new insight into the story of Natural Tunnel, it contains a superb wood engraving of a view from the South Portal, probably the best of all engravings of the 19th century (see Figure 17). An interior view is also included (see Figure 18).

THE NATURAL TUNNEL—LOOKING OUT.

Figure 16. This engraving by Van Ingen and Snyder is from Edward Pollard's *The Virginia Tourist*, 1871. This view in this engraving looks out of the South Portal and stretches the roof to allow a view of the Eagles Nest.

Also in 1874, *Scribners Monthly Magazine* published Edward King's "The Great South: A Ramble in Virginia," one of a series of travelogues. The following year, King's collection of articles was published in book form. His description of the Tunnel is brief (it is unlikely he visited it), though he does mention Bowlin Cave.

Charles B. Coale published his enigmatic book *The*

NATURAL TUNNEL.

Figure 17. Probably the best of 19th-century engravings of Natural Tunnel, this engraving is from *Picturesque America*, 1874. Compare this view to others out of the South Portal, and it is apparent, through time, engravers were working from the same original sketch. Note the repetition of certain trees when comparing the different engravings.

Life and Adventures of Wilburn Waters in 1878. The chapter entitled "The Natural Bridge of Scott" is little more than a telling of the human-pendulum story.

By this time in the 19th century, real progress, albeit slow, was being made toward a railroad opening up access to the Tunnel. With more and more activity in that regard, the Tunnel as a separate subject in literature waned, and it became more and more identified with the coming railroad. The days of the intrepid tourist were coming to an end. No longer would the traveler have to suffer the travails of the trail and the bed lice of Estillville, or be marooned in a dry county after a long horseback ride. One could pack his own bottle in his grip for the ride—by rail—to the Tunnel.

SIDE TRAIL

An idea of the size of some of the trees seen by the earliest visitors to the Tunnel is supplied by an editorial note to Long's 1832 article. He mentions the "Sycamore Camp" about a mile upstream from the North Portal, about which the editor states, "This designation has been given to the spot in the valley of the creek, where formerly stood a hollow sycamore (*platanus occidentalis*) tree of an enormous size, the remains of which are still to be seen, and in the cavity of which, whilst it stood, fifteen persons are said to have encamped at the same time together."

Interior of Natural Tunnel.

Figure 18. This engraving, also from *Picturesque America,* is almost an exact copy of *Harper's New Monthly Magazine*'s interior view.

SALTPETER AND "GENERAL" SALLING
MINING IN AND AROUND NATURAL TUNNEL, 1812-1865

NATURAL TUNNEL WAS MINED FOR SALTPETER AND ACCORDING TO PETER HAUER (PERS. COMM.) THE MINING WAS PROBABLY DONE ON THE SIDE OPPOSITE STOCK CREEK ABOVE THE RAILROAD TRACKS. ALTHOUGH EVERYTHING IS NOW COATED WITH SOOT FROM STEAM ENGINE DAYS, DRY PETRE DIRT WAS NOTED AT THE ABOVE MENTIONED SPOT BENEATH THE SOOT.

—JOHN R. HOLSINGER, 1971

or settlers in America, caves were an important source for obtaining saltpeter, an essential ingredient in gunpowder. Some parts of the cave environment allow for the formation of nitrates, particularly nitrocalcite (calcium nitrate). This material occurs in microscopic form in some cave earths, called "peter dirt," and during the 18th and 19th centuries, considerable effort occurred in the eastern United States to recover this material from caves.

Once mined, the peter dirt was flooded with water in a container and allowed to set for a few days. The water was then drained off. This leach-water, containing calcium nitrate, was then mixed with wood ashes or a leach-water from the wood ashes, which contained potassium hydroxide. Chemical exchange would occur between the two solutions, resulting in the formation of potassium nitrate—saltpeter—which was then recovered by evaporation, with the saltpeter remaining as fine crystals after the liquid was boiled off. The saltpeter would then be mixed with charcoal and sulfur, all finely ground (but not together at the same time!), to make gunpowder.

Most of the readily accessible caves in Southwest Virginia were likely at least prospected for peter dirt, and many were actively mined. Natural Tunnel seems an unlikely place for recovery of peter dirt, as it is a tunnel, not a cave, and is subject not only to wide temperature and humidity variations, but, having a stream running through it, flooding as well, which would wash away any accumulated peter dirt.

But in a letter to the editor of *The Southern Literary Messenger* in 1844, the writer, listed only as "W. H. C.," notes, "The material of which this stupendous fabric is composed [he is describing the rock forming the Tunnel] is a whitish limestone, strongly impregnated with saltpeter. The saltpeter was formerly collected in large quantities for the purpose of making gunpowder. I saw large heaps of earthy matter from which the nitre had been extracted." In this letter we are also introduced for the first time to the story of Poor Dotson, swinging perilously from an unraveling rope in his search for peter dirt.

The Reverend C. Collins, who visited the Tunnel about the same time as W. H. C., recounts his version of the Dotson story in his article "Virginia's Two Bridges" in an 1855 *The Ladies Repository*: "About the time of the last war, when salt peter was manufactured from the nitrous earth formed beneath the tunnel. . . ." The indicated conflict would most likely have been the War of 1812.

The South Atlantic and Ohio Railroad, in a promotional book issued in 1890, just after completion of the line, asserts, "About 1810-1812, when this commodity was much needed for the making of gunpowder for the impending war with England, scores of saltpeter works were set up in the nearby valley, and the Stock Creek tunnel was worked for material."

There are a number of openings in the Amphitheater wall, as well as the Shelter Caves, which could serve as the source of the heaps observed by W. H. C., so his observations do not prove recovery occurred from the Tunnel. In later years, Peter M. Hauer reported in *Descriptions of Virginia Caves* some evidence of mining for saltpeter, probably on the eastern side of the Tunnel, and John R. Holsinger found dry peter dirt at this point. The nearby Bowlin Cave and Natural Tunnel Caverns show signs of excavation, but likely not for saltpeter.

But probably the most convincing evidence that peter dirt was recovered from the Tunnel and was used to manufacture gunpowder comes from an astonishing source—the man who mined it himself during the Civil War, "General" John Salling, Virginia's last surviving Confederate veteran. (See Figure 19).

In 1954, G. Alexander Robertson interviewed "General" Salling for the *National Speleological Society News*. At that time, Mr. Salling was 106 years old and one of only five remaining Civil War veterans. These surviving gentlemen had the honorary title "General" conferred on them (Mr. Salling was never more than a lowly private).

Born in 1846 in the community of Slant near Natural Tunnel on the Clinch River, General Salling was a teenager when he joined the Confederate Army and was attached to the 25th Virginia Regiment.

Salling never served combat duty, but rather was put into service digging saltpeter to supply the Confederate Army—a duty for which he never received pay. To the Civil War buff and admirer of Natural Tunnel, interviewer Robinson's statement that General Salling mined saltpeter "for the Confederacy at the time of the battle of Gettysburg" is a succinct and moving phrase.

When asked by Robertson how he knew where to dig for saltpeter, Salling replied, "I didn't know—I just dug where they told me."

General Salling died in March of 1959 at the age of 112. A monument to him was erected near his home on the Clinch River (see Figure 20). There was, and still is, some question as to whether General Salling truly served during the Civil War, but in lieu of written documentation by an observer of saltpeter digging in the Tunnel, his statements tend to support the historical literary record and modern observations. And by any other standard, it's a great story.

Figure 19. "General" John Salling, in black coat, age 104, with his arm around "General" William J. Bush, oldest living Georgia veteran, in Confederate uniform, age 105, at the 61st, and final, reunion of the United Confederate Veterans in 1951. Mr. Salling mined saltpeter in Natural Tunnel for the 25th Virginia Regiment—at the same time as the Battle of Gettysburg. (From the Norfolk Public Library)

SIDE TRAILS

Three side trails deserve their own description here. Mrs. Ruby Stewart, granddaughter to E. H. Walker, one-time owner of Natural Tunnel, remembers interviewing Mr. Salling in the 1930s, when she worked in social services. While expressing her own reservations as to Mr. Salling's authenticity, she recalls that, when the movie *Gone With the Wind* premiered in 1939, Mr. Salling was dressed in a Confederate uniform and taken to the opening in Johnson City, Tennessee, as the guest of honor.

Mr. Salling attended the 75th anniversary of the Battle of Gettysburg in 1938. He traveled to that affair by automobile. He planned to travel to the final reunion of the United Confederate Veterans in 1951 the same way. However, a week before his trip, he came down with a cold and did not think he could make the long trip to Norfolk by car.

A flurry of phone calls by friends and concerned individuals resulted in an arrangement whereby a Navy transport aircraft picked up Mr. Salling at the Tri-Cities Airport in Tennessee for the trip, where he remarked it would be the first time he had ever been higher than High Knob. (High Knob is the highest point on Powell Mountain in Wise County, north of Natural Tunnel.) The following month, September 1951, Mr. Salling was commissioned a colonel in the Confederate Air Force and made acting commander of the Army of Northern Virginia Department.

Figure 20. Monument to General Salling erected by the Virginia Division of the United Daughters of the Confederacy, May 15, 1961, near his home at Slant, Virginia.

Mr. Jimmy Frazier, also kin to the Walker family, recalls picking up Mr. Salling in an ambulance, taking him to Gate City, and driving him in May Day parades. But most interestingly, at the time of Mr. Salling's death, Jimmy was the youngest funeral director in the Commonwealth of Virginia, and the last to bury a coffin—containing Mr. Salling—covered by the Stars and Bars.

A RAILROAD WILL RUN THROUGH IT
DEVELOPING THE RAILROAD, 1848-1890

IN A FEW YEARS, IT IS CONFIDENTLY EXPECTED, A RAILROAD WILL FIND ITS WAY THROUGH THIS WONDERFUL TUNNEL, AND THE LOCOMOTIVE'S SCREAM WILL BE HEARD ON THE PATH OVER WHICH DANIEL BOONE PAINFULLY TOILED, MORE THAN A CENTURY AGO, ON HIS PIONEERING PILGRIMAGE TO THE KENTUCKY WILDS.

—EDWARD KING, 1874

atural Tunnel and the railroad running through it are like bourbon and branch water; wonderful in their own right, but something more wonderful still when mixed. It is difficult now, if not impossible, to speak of the Tunnel without the phrase "a railroad runs through it" entering the conversation. The combination is a big draw for the railfan. The sight of big Norfolk Southern diesel-electric engines pulling a hundred-car coal train with a "rumble and a roar," the ground vibrating and the horn echoing off the Amphitheater walls, is a thrill for the novice and aficionado alike. Better yet, on those rare occasions when an old steam engine, dusted and polished fresh from the shop, pulls an excursion train through the Tunnel, no one can look on without wishing for the chance to be "behind the stack."

Can you imagine the hue and cry if, today, a railroad proposed putting its line through one of the greatest karst features in the world? It wouldn't, and shouldn't, happen. That is not to say the fact that a railroad line now runs through Natural Tunnel is a bad thing. It simply does, and now they complement each other. In earlier times, no one gave it a second thought—except for one man we should be thankful for. His part in the story is just one of the many wheels-within-wheels that constitute Natural Tunnel's railroad history.

As noted earlier, one would think that Natural Tunnel's railroad story would start with Lieutenant Colonel Long, a great early railroad figure, but he was thinking of a simple wagon road. The story begins in 1848, with the organization of the Lynchburg & Tennessee Railroad, which changed its name to the Virginia & Tennessee Railroad the following year. This line, completed to Bristol in 1856, would be an important lifeline for the Confederacy during the Civil War.

In 1852, just shortly after its organization, the V&T was looking to branch into Lee, Scott, and Russell counties (Wise County would be formed from parts of these three in 1856), both to access the iron deposits there and to link with the Kentucky railroad systems and thus be another route west, over and through the Appalachians, providing a route between Norfolk, Virginia, and Louisville, Kentucky. Charles F. M. Garnett, chief engineer of the V&T, was in charge of a reconnaissance survey of a route from Abingdon to the Cumberland Gap made by an assistant, a Mr. Gardner. The resulting map (See Figure 6) plainly shows Natural Tunnel essential to that path.

In a report dated October 31, 1853, included with the V&T annual report, Garnett states, "The singular beauty of the scenery on this line would make it a popular route. The natural tunnel in Scott county and the large and beautiful cave in the same neighborhood are considerations which would make it a popular route."

On March 3, 1852, the Virginia General Assembly authorized the V&T to build a branch line to the Cumberland Gap, but the legislature also specified that if not built, the right to do so could pass to another company. The V&T did not follow through, probably because its hands were full simply building the main line. In 1853, interested Southwest Virginians organized the Virginia & Kentucky Railroad (V&K) and took on the route, with Virginia offering $1,500,000 out of the state treasury if the Kentucky legislature would adopt measures to ensure continuance of the line through that state.

William Beverhout Thompson, chief engineer for the V&K, resurveyed the line "following generally the route formerly surveyed by Col. Garnette." In a report dated March 15, 1859, to the company's board of directors, Thompson states, "The admirers of nature will doubtless be attracted to the locality when the way shall have been provided for visiting it. It will require comparatively but little work to pre-

pare it for the passage of the Locomotive and will save to the company many thousands of dollars."

By 1861, only 10 to 20 miles had been graded westward out of Bristol. An audit by the Commonwealth of Virginia found that, in the confusing array of financing, the state was paying the entire cost of construction, with the contractor milking the cash payments (a by-no-means-unheard-of practice in railroad building). The state's refusal to continue payment caused operations to be suspended. Of course, the onset of the Civil War stopped any further consideration of railroad construction.

In the years 1866 through 1868, V&K President Robert William Hughes, prominent lawyer and unsuccessful Republican candidate for Virginia governor, pleaded the case of the need for the V&K, citing the abundant iron-ore resources of the area the line would penetrate (an exaggeration, but a widely held belief at the time), its strategic location as a connector with the eastern and midwestern United States (still true, but even more so in those days, when freight and passenger service was more critical), and the abundant coal resources (here he hit the nail on the head).

In 1866, at a meeting of the railroad organizers, Hughes urged them to again take hold of the project, proclaiming the route beckoned its builders, saying, "The very mountains, instead of frowning upon and opposing us, seem to invite us to make this road. The Clinch sinks down and disappears for its passage. The Natural tunnel and Creek Valley present themselves for the transit through Purchase Ridge."

In 1867, Mr. Hughes continued his crusade to revive the road in an article in *Debow's Review*, noting, "The fact has not yet attracted much public notice in Virginia, that the new State of West Virginia came near depriving Virginia of all her coal measures. She took with her 15,900 square miles of the finest coal measures in the world . . . leaving to Virginia no portion of her magnificent carboniferous domain except the triangle of territory embracing [Lee, Wise, Scott, Buchanan, Russell, and Tazewell] counties." Ultimately, the coal left in "Ol' Virginny" would drive the building of the road.

In 1868, Hughes gave one more try. At the Bristol Convention, attended by "many of the first men of Virginia and Tennessee, those of the latter preponderating in numbers," Hughes again made his pitch. Those attending the convention wanted to find a way to tie the Eastern Seaboard, with its many ports and particularly Norfolk, to the Midwest and West via railroads (the Union Pacific and Central Pacific were racing toward each other at this time).

Of course, Mr. Hughes pointed out the strategic location of his line; in the September issue of *Debow's Review*, the recorder of the convention states, "The resolutions of Colonel Hughes, the President of the Virginia and Kentucky railroad, touch upon a subject of vast importance to Norfolk, viz: the connection between our city and the northwest. Our citizens have not devoted their thoughts sufficiently to this subject."

Mr. Hughes's pleas came to naught. His push for the rail line came only three years after the "Recent Unpleasantness"; the South's economy lay in shambles, and while many were interested, none were financially capable. The V&K languished.

In 1869, the Virginia & Tennessee Railroad consolidated with the Norfolk and Petersburg Railroad, the Southside Railroad, and the floundering Virginia & Kentucky to form the Atlantic, Mississippi and Ohio Railroad—the precursor to the mighty Norfolk and Western Railway. In procuring the charter for his company, Major General William Mahone, president of the company, induced the state to allow him to mortgage the entire line, agreeing that a sum of $4,500,000 be set aside to complete the old V&K line. Mahone obviously had no intentions to do so, using the V&K ploy to increase his cash flow. After making some rudimentary demonstrations toward completion of the line—primarily some preliminary engineering work—in 1874 he got an act passed through the Virginia legislature releasing the Atlantic, Mississippi and Ohio from that obligation until Kentucky held up its end of the deal, which, again, did not happen.

Enter the locals. On October 27, 1875, a meeting was held in the store of William W. James, the "prince merchant," in Goodson (later Bristol), Virginia. W. W. James was the pivotal figure in these early days of Natural Tunnel, and his story deserves its own account later. But for now, he and a number of other prominent merchants, politicians, and capitalists met to take up the reins abandoned by Mr. Hughes, to finally make the road. Those in attendance at this meeting included many great figures in the history of Southwest Virginia and the as-yet-undreamed-of town of Big Stone Gap. Present were Henry Clinton Wood (or Clint Wood, whose name was given to that town in Dickenson County), Patrick Hagan, Rufus A. Ayers, Isaac C. Fowler, William D. Jones, and many others.

All of these men wanted the road in the worst sort of way. Why? While their prospectus and exhortatory letters emphasized how landowners would benefit from soaring land values, those documents did not point out what the merchants and politicians wanted—profit and power. They saw in this enterprise the chance to open new ground and new markets, to be empire builders. While certainly not on the same scale as the transcontinental railroad, they had the same opportunity—to be the first and to reap the rewards. They all bought shares in the company, at $20 each, with Scott County and the Town of Bristol-Goodson holding the lion's share.

On March 27, 1876, the Virginia General Assembly passed the rights of the V&K to build a railroad to the Cumberland Gap to the new company, the Bristol Coal and Iron Narrow Gauge Railway (hereafter referred to as the NG). This time, the starting point would be Bristol-Goodson, not Abingdon. Henry C. Wood was elected president of the company, W. W. James vice-president, and Colonel J. M. Barker secretary and treasurer (later replaced by John F. Terry).

W. W. James wasted no time. A day spent in the deed-book room of the Scott County Courthouse, tracing Mr. James's path buying up the right-of-way along the line, shows a man who knew what his company needed and what he, personally, wanted. Marching along, he obtained rights one after the other for the NG, until he paused in the vicinity of Natural Tunnel. He then proceeded to buy up the Tunnel and its northern and southern approaches for himself and his partners, I. C. Fowler and W. D. Jones! (It seems the old V&K had been a bit lax in obtaining right-of-way, and its entire line was trespassing! The NG line coincided with the old V&K line at a few points.)

Ground was broken for the line in August of 1879, with W. W. James turning over the first shovelful of dirt to fanfare and speeches. Off the crew marched, composed mostly of convicts "requisitioned" by Henry C. Wood, building the line west out of Bristol with Chief Engineer L. Chalmers King and his assistant, Thomas Bibb, scouting the way.

Less than a year later, work slowed down, due to a lack of working capital. In August of 1880, the Tinsalia Coal & Iron Company (TC&IC) subscribed to enough stock in the company to both keep it going and hold controlling interest. The company put their representative, General John Imboden, in control of the project. The TC&IC, headed by Pittsburgh capitalists A. O. and C. S. O. Tinstman, who were looking to expand into the rich mineral resources of Southwest Virginia, meant its investment to be a stopgap measure, intending to raise sufficient capital by a bond issue. But the bond issue never happened, and the convict labor continued.

Just as in the heyday of the transcontinental railroad race, with major American papers reporting daily progress, I. C. Fowler, editor of the *Bristol News* and later part owner of the Tunnel, reported on the progress of the NG:

September 14, 1880. "Capt. King's engineering corps will go on the line beyond Speer's Ferry tomorrow. The most difficult engineering will be in passing the Natural Tunnel. Gen. Imboden will have the 22 miles from Clinch river to the gap let to contract as soon as it can be located and it will be finished early next year. . . ."

September 28, 1880. "Capt. King's corps is now locating the line from Speer's Ferry to Stone Gap. He thinks the line will pass just to the left of the Natural Tunnel. If so, the lower end of the tunnel will be invisible from the cars, but the upper end will be in fine view. . . ."

[*Note:* While not reported in the paper, on October 15, 1880, James, Jones, and Fowler purchased the Tunnel and bounding land from four separate families.]

October 19, 1880. "Mr. James, general superintendent of the NGRR, returned last week from Scott, and reports a beautiful line located from Speer's Ferry as far as the Natural Tunnel. The line runs the tunnel and it will interfere with that great work very little, it is hoped—that is, the walls will be cut but little. . . .

"Supt. James and Dr. Hilton have obtained the right of way from nearly every man between Speer's Ferry and Natural Tunnel. Signed, sealed and acknowledged. That's business! The engineer and the Pittsburgh gentlemen [the new backers of the railroad] say they must put the road through the Natural Tunnel. The eastern supporting wall of the arch of the Tunnel at its lower extremity protrudes outward into the tunnel some 12 feet. They said that to reduce this to its perpendicular will be the only cutting necessary to that wonderful natural curiosity. I hope so. The located line crosses Stock Creek near its mouth and passes up the eastern side of it all the way to the tunnel without crossing it. There will be four crossings in and about the tunnel. [Revealingly, Editor Fowler finishes with the crux of the matter.] In twelve months we shall be rid of the Knoxville Coal Ring. We shall have better coal and greatly cheaper coal. . . ."

November 2, 1880. "Capt. Ed Winston, one of the finest and most experienced engineers in the country, has succeeded the lamented King as chief engineer, and is now equipped with a splendid corps, which has completed the location of the western section to a point two miles north of the great Natural Tunnel, through which the line passes without any mutilation. . . ."

An exciting and heady time, but any reader of early railroad history, or this history for that matter, knows what came next—financial difficulties. By 1881, with the line essentially located, work on the grade had stopped, due to the simple lack of capital.

E. K. Hyndman, vice-president and managing director of the TC&IC, had been aggressively (cannily, perhaps?) pushing the development of the company in Southwest Virginia—so aggressively, in fact, that the Tinstmans grew uneasy. They sold their interests in the company and the railroad to Hyndman. Hyndman turned right around and approached Judge John Leisenring and associates of Mauch Chunk, Pennsylvania, offering to sell the company's holdings, which included vast mineral lands and, of course, the railroad.

A new company, the Virginia Coal and Iron Company (VC&IC), was formed, with its charter granted by the Virginia legislature on January 6, 1882. (The original organizers are well-known names in Southwest Virginia, including John and E. B. Leisenring, J. S. Wentz, and J. F. Bullitt. These names would figure prominently as this company evolved into the Westmoreland Coal Company.) The NG's name was changed to the South Atlantic and Ohio (SA&O) by act of the Virginia General Assembly on January 26, 1882, succeeding to all the rights of the former company. The VC&IC was determined to push the building of the road—development of the mineral properties would demand it—but, after organization, capital was again wanting for completion.

Enter Dr. J. M. Bailey. Dr. Bailey (what type doctor is unknown, but it seems he rose to a modicum of fame as a practitioner of ensilage on his farm in Massachusetts), with backing by Boston bankers, took over control of the floundering railroad company and got it moving, this time as a standard gauge. The exact organization of the new company is unclear, but it is clear that the VC&IC, major stockholder of the SA&O, entered into an agreement with Dr. Bailey, whereby Bailey purchased the entire VC&IC railroad stock. Soon after, Bailey organized the Bailey Construction Company—with his Boston backers—and as president of the company, started building.

By 1887, the road was graded to Estillville and track laid a short distance beyond Mendota. It is interesting to note that the first mortgage of the SA&O in 1886 was through the American Loan and Trust Company of Boston—again, it would appear creative financing in railroad construction was reaping somebody the profit!

Interlude. In 1882, a momentous happening in the history of the Tunnel occurred. W. W. James (and wife) and W. D. Jones (and wife) conveyed to the SA&O Railroad the right to construct a railroad bed through their tunnel, the Natural Tunnel. But the deed had a stipulation: "the said railroad company is further to remove all materials, such as dirt . . . not used in constructing their roadbed to a convenient distance from the mouth of said tunnel . . . to conduct their work . . . in a prudent and careful manner, so as not to mar or disfigure the natural appearance of said tunnel more than will occasionally result from building their road." The present appearance of the Tunnel is owed to the James and Jones concern, even if it was tainted with more than a bit of profit in mind.

Bailey got the company moving. By February of 1887 (see Figure 21), passengers could board the train at Bristol and ride to Mendota, a grand total of fifteen miles in one hour and twenty minutes.

In the spring of 1887, negotiations opened between the stockholders of the Bailey Construction Company and a group of New York financiers, including John H. Inman, later of Wise County coal fame. The result was the Virginia, Tennessee & Carolina Steel & Iron Company (VT&CS&IC). Bailey Construction Company sold its entire holdings to the VT&CS&IC, for cash and stockholdings in the new company.

Bailey went to work again, but something—it's unclear what—went wrong. The management of the VT&CS&IC grew dissatisfied with Bailey's management and apparently threw him out on his ear. The October 1887 timetable (see Figure 22) shows that you could depart Bristol, passing the "Chalybeate Springs" (present-day Maces Spring, then a "medicinal stop" for the chalybeate water) and make it to Estillville two hours and 31.5 miles later but not quite make it to the Marble Quarries (the name given to excavations of the red-hued limestones still seen today in the vicinity of Gate City). But Bailey had been replaced by H. W. Bates. There was bad blood there, and Bailey had a score to settle. The situation would come back to haunt the company.

Would this poor little railroad ever make it to Big Stone Gap? Little information regarding the status of the railroad from 1887 to 1889 has been found, and it appears plausible the turmoil caused a temporary cessation of construction until 1889, when work finally restarted. This time the line would make it. But first it had to run the Tunnel.

SIDE TRACK

Bob Pannell, born in 1898, was the son of a blacksmith and wagonmaker whose family name was given to the cave beside Stock Creek now referred to as Natural Tunnel Caverns. The foundation of the

SOUTH ATLANTIC AND OHIO RAILROAD.

H. C. Wood, President.	J. Wilder, Gen. Freight Agent.
John M. Bailey, Gen. Manager.	Geo. A. Blackmore,
John L. Wellington, Supt.	Gen. Ticket Agent.

General Offices—Bristol, Tenn.

February 15, 1887.	Mls	No. 1 Mail.
Lve. **Bristol**	0	8 40 A.M.
" Walker's Mountain....	4.5	9 05 "
" Benham	7.5	9 20 "
" Abram's Falls	12.0	l 9 40 "
" Mendota	15.0	10 00 A.M.
" Chalybeate Springs	20.0	
" Hilton	24.5	
" Mocassin Gap	29.0	
" Estillville	31.5	
" Marble Quarries	36.5	
Arr. **Clinch River**	41.5	

STATIONS.	Mls	No. 2 Mail.
Lve. **Clinch River**	0	
" Marble Quarries	5.0	
" Estillville	10.0	
" Mocassin Gap	12.5	
" Hilton	17.5	
" Chalybeate Springs	22.0	
" Mendota	27.0	4 00 P.M.
" Abram's Falls	30.0	4 20 "
" Benham	34.5	5 00 "
" Walker's Mountain	37.5	5 30 "
Arr. **Bristol**	41.5	5 50 P.M.

STANDARD—*Central time.*   *l* Stops only to leave passengers.

CONNECTIONS.—At Bristol—With Norfolk & Western R.R. for Richmond, Washington, Philadelphia, New York and Norfolk, Va. With East Tennessee, Virginia & Georgia R.R. for Knoxville, Chattanooga and Atlanta.

Trains arrive at Bristol, via Norfolk & Western R.R., 2 20, 9 05 a.m. Leave at 6 50 a.m., 9 30 p.m. (*Eastern time.*)

Trains arrive, via East Tennessee, Virginia & Georgia R.R. (*Central time*), 5 45 a.m., 8 20 p.m. Trains leave 1 30, 8 20 a.m.

The *South Atlantic & Ohio Railroad* is in process of construction to the *"Breaks" in the Cumberland Mountain,* 120 miles. Will be open to *Estillville* in April, and to the *Clinch River* in May, 42 miles. To *Big Stone Gap* in 1887, and to the *"Breaks"* in 1888.

SOUTH ATLANTIC AND OHIO RAILROAD.

Nathaniel Thayer, President.	W. C. Harrington,
H. W. Bates, Vice-President.	Gen. Freight & Passenger Agent.
T. H. Wentworth, Secretary.	John Jenkins, Superintendent.

General Offices—Bristol, Tenn.

October 5, 1887.	Mls	No. 1 Mail.	No. 3
Lve. **Bristol**	0	10 00 A.M.	4 00 P.M.
" Walker's Mountain. ...	4.5	10 18 "	4 18 "
" Benham's	7.5	10 28 "	4 28 "
" Abram's Falls	12.0	10 50 "	4 50 "
" Mendota	15.0	11 00 "	4 58 "
" Mace Springs	20.0	11 17 "	5 17 "
" Hilton's	24.5	11 34 "	5 34 "
" Mocassin Gap	29.0	11 50 A.M.	5 50 "
" Estillville	31.5	12 00 NO'N	6 00 P.M.
" Marble Quarries	36.5		
Arr. **Clinch River**	41.5		

STATIONS.	Mls	No. 2 Mail.	No. 4
Lve. **Clinch River**	0		
" Marble Quarries	5.0		
" Estillville	10.0	8 00 A.M.	4 00 P.M.
" Mocassin Gap	12.5	8 10 "	4 10 "
" Hilton's	17.5	8 26 "	4 26 "
" Mace Springs	22.0	8 42 "	4 42 l
" Mendota	27.0	8 58 "	4 58 "
" Abram's Falls	30.0	9 08 "	5 08 "
" Benham's	34.5	9 30 "	5 30 "
" Walker's Mountain. ...	37.5	9 40 "	5 40 "
Arr. **Bristol**	41.5	10 00 A.M.	6 00 P.M.

STANDARD—*Central time.*   *l* Stops only to leave passengers.

CONNECTIONS.—At Bristol—With Norfolk & Western R.R. for Richmond, Washington, Philadelphia, New York and Norfolk, Va. With East Tennessee, Virginia & Georgia R.R. for Knoxville, Chattanooga and Atlanta.

Trains arrive at Bristol, via Norfolk & Western R.R., 9 05 a.m., 12 15 noon. Leave at 7 25 a.m., 8 20 p.m. (*Eastern time.*)

Trains arrive, via East Tennessee, Virginia & Georgia R.R. (*Central time*), 6 20 a.m., 7 10 p.m. Trains leave 8 20 a.m., 11 45 p.m.

The *South Atlantic & Ohio Railroad* is in process of construction to the *"Breaks" in the Cumberland Mountain,* 120 miles. Will be open to *Big Stone Gap* in 1888.

Figure 21. The February 15, 1887, timetable for the SA&O shows a grand total of fifteen miles passable in one hour and twenty minutes. At that time, Henry C. Wood was president of the company and John M. Bailey general manager. The company would soon reorganize, and management would change. Note the company's statement that they were in the process of constructing a line to the Breaks (on the Virginia-Kentucky border). They would never make it. (Timetable from the John Dale collection)

Figure 22. The October 5, 1887, timetable for the SA&O shows 31.5 miles of track open, passable in two hours, and that J. M Bailey has been replaced by H. W. Bates. While still claiming to be constructing a line to the Breaks on the Virginia-Kentucky border, the company has moved its arrival at Big Stone Gap from 1887 to 1888. The line would take a while longer. (Timetable from the John Dale collection)

Pannell homeplace can still be seen at a resurgent spring on the north bank of Stock Creek. In 1971, the first Natural Tunnel State Park manager, Gil Bledsoe, spoke with Mr. Pannell, who remembered (probably via his father's recollection) that, until the line was completed through the Tunnel, a turntable existed at Glenita to turn the SA&O engines. Later, when the Virginia & Southwestern Railway put larger engines on the line, a wye (a "Y" shaped track arrangement to allow an engine to turn) was constructed in the hollow below the Devil's Racepath (the name for the twisting path over Purchase Ridge to Duffield). This wye was likely short-lived; a 1918 photograph does not show one present.

THE WOULD-BE EMPIRE OF W. W. JAMES

THE FIRST ATTEMPT AT DEVELOPMENT, 1875-1889

et us be sure of one thing; William Walter James was a businessman's businessman, and the profit motive was strong in him. But his desire for money seems to have been tempered by a moral heart, with a soft spot in it for a special place—Natural Tunnel. For that special place, he would try to reconcile the conflict between business and preservation.

W. W. James started his merchant career in Blountville, Tennessee, around 1845, and by 1855 he was part owner of a store in Bristol, Virginia, though he still operated his Blountville enterprise. The loss of his original store, by fire, during the Battle of Blountville on September 22, 1863, caused him to abandon that town. Blountville's loss was Bristol's boon.

Bud Phillips's book, *Bristol Tennessee/Virginia, A History—1852-1900,* is full of references to W. W. James. James's magnanimous nature and civic-mindedness earned him the sobriquet, via Mr. Phillips, of the "prince merchant." His short but concise summary of James's life is as follows: "In time he became the leading merchant on the Virginia side of town. He long was at the forefront of the civic leaders of Bristol, helped to form the second bank of Bristol, Virginia, did much real estate developing, and strongly supported the building of area railroads. He played a leading role in the establishment of Sullins College, so much so that it was almost called James College. . . ." For his part in the story of Natural Tunnel, the operative words in the previous statement are "real estate" and "railroads."

How Mr. James came to know of Natural Tunnel

is uncertain. Certainly, he lived in nearby Blountville, his second wife was from Southwest Virginia, and in his business dealings and through conversation with locals, he would have heard of it. As we have seen before, through his position with the old Bristol Coal and Iron Narrow Gauge Railway, if he did not have firsthand knowledge of the Tunnel, he was at least aware of it, as it lay on the path of that railroad. And when he saw it, he bought it—even though he was ostensibly purchasing right-of-way for the railroad. In fairness to Mr. James, this practice was common in the early days of railroad building and is certainly not uncommon in other businesses, even today.

James didn't go it alone. As partners in his purchase, Mr. James enlisted W. D. Jones, another Bristol merchant and occasional business associate (whose monetary role in the affair may have been greater than can be recognized by the record), and Isaac C. Fowler, editor of the *Bristol News*. These gentlemen were connected with the old Narrow Gauge Railway, and they obviously were good friends with Mr. James, and of like mind. They had something up their sleeves, but what? First, the purchase.

Tracing the ownership of Natural Tunnel, though not an easy task, is reasonably straightforward back to the entrance of James and company on the scene. At that point, the concept of Natural Tunnel, as a piece of real estate, appears as if by magic. Backwards in time from then, there seems to be no one deed, no one piece of paper that states who owned the Tunnel. With gratitude to Emile Low, the reason why is now clear—no one did! In his 1893 article on the Tunnel, Low ends, "It may be stated in conclusion that the tunnel was a noted 'corner' for several tracts of land, the survey for each of which called for its inclusion. This made it extremely difficult to establish its exact ownership. In 1880, however, it was purchased by Messrs. James, Fowler and Jones of Bristol, Tenn. . . ."

The summary by Mr. Low explains the confusing deed for the Tunnel property. This deed, dated October 15, 1880, was between the sellers, William P. and Emily Good, Martin and Eliza Hill, Jesse and Jane Bishop, and Charles and Esther Horton, and the buyers, James, Fowler, and Jones. Apparently all the sellers claimed at least a part (if not all) of the Tunnel within their property line. James and company solved this problem by definitely carving out the Tunnel into a separate piece of property, ending that dispute.

The buyers paid $950 for 70 acres of land. Why they bought the property is also shown by the deed. A stipulation in the deed says that William Good may build a mill dam and race if he agreed "to furnish a good Road way over his mill Race & over his land around the Mill Dam for the use of said James & Fowler & Jones and all persons visiting the Natural Tunnel at all times by permission of said James & Fowler & Jones their heirs or assigns." James, Fowler, and Jones wanted in the tourist trade. After all, a railroad—one of which they were all stockholders—was coming.

In retrospect, it is obvious now why Editor Fowler, in his *Bristol News,* made it a point to mention the Tunnel in his writings on the progress of the NG and as a separate item of reportage. He was drumming up interest in the James and company endeavor.

In the August 17, 1880, issue of the *Bristol News,* Fowler describes a visit to the Tunnel the previous month by an 18-person party from Bristol, including Mr. James and Mr. Fowler, their wives, and a photographer, G. B. Smith. (It is interesting to note that some of the party, both going and coming, stayed with Mr. William Speer, then operating his namesake ferry). Fowler spends considerable space describing the Tunnel and then ends by stating that the pictures Mr. Smith took could be purchased at his gallery or the *News* office (these pictures have yet to be located if they still exist) and that "Next year this party, so charmed with the romantic scenery of a trip to the Natural Tunnel, hope to visit it again, but as passengers on the Narrow Gauge R. R." As it turned out, some of that party visited the Tunnel even before then—and bought it!

In the May 24, 1881, issue, Fowler wrote, "Messrs. James and Fowler returned last week from the Natural Tunnel, where they laid off the coming town of Jamesville. In a few weeks they will be ready to furnish lots, and already they have a number of applications. Main, or Tunnel, Street will be precisely north and south. Until the exact location of the depot building is known it will be difficult to adjust the prices of lots."

Jamesville! So it would seem that Mr. James had a little more in mind than simply controlling access to the Tunnel for the tourist trade. This consummate businessman wanted a bit of immortality by having a town named after him, not unlike many of the (later) coal barons. The exact location of this town of Jamesville—and for that matter, Tunnel Street—is uncertain, though given the description of the property, it likely would have been the present site of the community of Glenita.

While James and company controlled the north and south accesses to the Tunnel, there is certainly no room for a community there. Besides his major purchase of the Tunnel, he also purchased various tracts in the vicinity, and many of the deeds for these tracts reference the community of Jamesville, though no record of incorporation has been found.

Let us not forget Mr. James's other ambition. On March 6, 1882, the Virginia General Assembly passed an act incorporating the Great Natural Bridge and Tunnel Company, with James, Fowler, and Jones, plus Elbert Fowler (brother to Isaac and co-owner of the *Bristol News*) as organizers. The company was authorized to issue stock; purchase and control real estate; build and operate hotels, bridges, electric lights, and elevators; charge fees of admission to its property; quarry and mine; construct railroad lines not to exceed five miles in length; and buy and sell goods and wares. The design of James and company was now obvious.

Such a design—a community and tourist attraction—could draw people only if access was easy (a problem that future owners would also face), and easy access required the railroad. By deed dated June 5, 1882, James, Jones, and their wives gave the SA&O right-of-way through the Tunnel. (Fowler is not listed in the document. See discussion below.)

The deed states, "the said railroad company shall have no further control of any portion of the premises. . . . The said parties of the first part [James and Jones] reserve the right to regulate access to said tunnel against all persons except travelers and officers upon the trains. . . . The said railroad company further obligates itself to establish a depot upon said premises on the tract of land conveyed to it by William P. Good, and agrees not to permit trains to stop and remain in, or at either end of the tunnel except in case of emergency necessarily requiring it, or when stopping at a platform which they agree to construct at such convenient points across the mouth of said tunnel as may be designated by the parties of the first part. The said railroad company is further to remove all materials, such as dirt, that may be blown off or excavated, and not used in constructing their roadbed to a convenient distance from the mouth of said tunnel, not to exceed one thousand feet, to be designated by the parties of the first part, and said railroad company agrees to conduct their work of construction through the Natural Tunnel upon the right-of-way thereby granted in a prudent and careful manner, so as not to mar or disfigure the natural appearance of said tunnel more than will occasionally result from building their road. The depot and office is to be completed simultaneously with the road. . . ."

Fowler continued his part in the design. In the June 20, 1882, issue of the *Bristol News,* he kept the Tunnel before his readership. "Fact, sir, and been a fact for two years, and when the SA&O Railroad [the old Narrow Gauge had been reorganized and renamed by this time] shall have been completed you may come and view it [obviously by paying a charge to the company!], and then see that it is incomparably superior to the Natural Bridge in Rockbridge. . . . When it becomes accessible, the world will wonder why it had not become famous at an earlier day. It is the grandest work in all Virginia."

Fowler didn't forget the value of public relations, both with his readership and his partners. In the summer of 1882, he published a glowing account of W. D. Jones, "who is widely and favorably known throughout this part of the country as one of the most wide-awake and enterprising young men that this country has produced . . . it will be seen that he is one of the owners of the great Natural Bridge and Tunnel, situated in Scott County, Virginia [*note:* so was Fowler!], forty miles from Bristol and one of the greatest natural curiosities of this country, and near which the SA&O is likely to pass. He is liberal to a fault, always willing to help the poor and needy. . . ." In the late 1860s, Jones had removed to Philadelphia and was likely the main contact for the Philadelphia financiers investing in the railroad.

In that same issue, Fowler published the organizational proceedings of the Great Natural Bridge and Tunnel Company. James, Jones, and Fowler each invested $5,000 in the company. They had their charter, they had invested their money, one of their clan could sway public interest with his paper, so. . . .

Nothing happened. Why? These men had bet on a dark horse, the railroad. By 1887, five years after deeding the right-of-way to the railroad—a long time to wait for a return on an investment—the line had made it only to Estillville, certainly not to "Jamesville." James still had his enterprises in Bristol and was doing quite well. However, his son and namesake, set up by his father as a Bristol merchant, apparently overextended his credit in that regard, and distraught, shot himself on March 12, 1888.

Fowler had entered politics, serving three consecutive terms in the Virginia legislature, one as Speaker of the House of Delegates (1881-1883). In 1884, he was appointed clerk of the federal court in Abingdon, and he gave up the newspaper business. W. D. Jones seems to have removed permanently to Philadelphia. These gentlemen had moved on. The dream had died.

On July 1, 1889, Fowler and his wife sold ⅓ interest in the Natural Tunnel property to the Virginia, Tennessee & Carolina Steel & Iron Company for

$3,026. On October 1, 1889, James and his wife conveyed the remainder of the property to the company for $12,000; the deed stipulated a pay-off to W. D. Jones for $4,000, with the remainder to go to James.

It would appear that James, Jones, and Fowler had come to some mutual agreement as to control of the property, perhaps through the Great Natural Bridge and Tunnel Company. The different dates of sale, along with the different selling prices and the observation that their wives had also come to be owners—not evident in the original deed—imply that other deed/agreements had been made, and might explain why Fowler had not been party to the right-of-way agreement.

Regardless, the grand scheme had failed. No Jamesville appeared, and certainly no Tunnel Street, and no hoards of eager tourists filed off the train. Yet these gentlemen, and James in particular, probably saved the Tunnel from disfigurement at the hooves of the iron horse. Rest assured, they were in it for the money, and it appears they may have made a little for their trouble, but they were also preservationists. In the final assessment, probably the most important thing these gentlemen did was carve out the Natural Tunnel and surrounding lands into a distinct and separate entity.

Now the time had come for the railroad to hold sway, at least for a while.

Side Entry

If there are heroes in the story of Natural Tunnel, W. W. James is certainly at the head of the list. The enigmatic W. D. Jones is likely on that list, too, but at present his exact role in the early ownership of Natural Tunnel is unclear. That he was the likely pivot point for financial matters in the first undisputed ownership of the Tunnel is hinted at in Editor Fowler's summer of 1882 article on Mr. Jones, where he states, "Acting upon his judgment and with the nerve necessary for such an undertaking, he converted quietly his accumulated means into mountain land lying in Letcher, Perry and Pike Counties, Kentucky, and the adjoining counties in Virginia, Wise, Scott and Lee, until now at this writing, he holds in fee simple, jointly with a prominent Philadelphia millionaire, upward of 200,000 acres of the richest land to be found in this country—rich both on the surface and below it."

HOW CONVENIENT, THIS PLACE

THE RAILROAD RUNS THROUGH THE TUNNEL, 1888-1890

THE NEW ROAD, WHICH WILL MAKE A PRAC-
TICAL USE OF THE TUNNEL, WILL RUN FROM
BRISTOL, TENN., TO BIG STONE GAP, VA., ON THE
KENTUCKY STATE LINE, A DISTANCE OF 80 MILES.
ABOUT 40 MILES OF IT HAVE BEEN GRADED, AND
IT IS UNDER CONTRACT TO BE FINISHED IN TWO
YEARS. HAD IT BEEN NECESSARY TO TUNNEL
THROUGH THE MOUNTAIN THE COMPANY MUST
HAVE SPENT AT LEAST $500,000.

—THE *PHILADELPHIA EVENING RECORD*,
REPRINTED IN *THE RAILROAD
GAZETTE*, SEPTEMBER 3, 1886

The Tunnel waited, as it had for nearly a million years, the perfect way through Purchase Ridge. Cross the main Clinch River at Speers Ferry and again at Clinchport, follow the Stock Creek Valley, pass through the Tunnel, a climbing grade to Horton's Summit, then down Hunter Valley to Duffield and on to Big Stone Gap. But first, the South Atlantic and Ohio had to figure out how to build a line up the chasm of Stock Creek and into and through a natural tunnel, pierced by a mountain stream with a tight S curve, too tight for the railroad to follow.

By 1889, construction was again in earnest. Most likely, with the proximity of wagon roads to the line, grading and construction was proceeding north and south of the Tunnel at the same time. Unlike some lines, especially those into unpopulated lands, such as the transcontinental railroad, the builders of the SA&O were not dependent on supplies for the railroad itself coming only by train to the end of track (certainly the grade work, predominantly manual labor, was not dependent on this method).

The person who holds the credit for the design of the construction to and through the Tunnel is unclear. Of course, fixing of the line can be traced from Charles F. M. Garnett of the V&T, to L. Chalmers King with the NG, to Edward Winston with the NG, to a "Captain Jones" mentioned in correspondence to Dr. Bailey with the SA&O. They were all gone, dead or displaced. Finally, the South Atlantic and Ohio was moving. They had to get through that Tunnel. Who would do it?

The record is a bit clouded as to who was in charge, most likely due to the continuing discord in SA&O management and an almost constant reorganization of the company (as was true with many of the new companies entering the Virginia coalfields at that time). Other engineers of record with the SA&O include J. J. Sickler and J. C. Oliphant (also involved in the early days of the Virginia Coal and Iron Company), but the credit falls, whether by fact or default, to J. H. McCue.

In the January 1944 issue of *Trains* magazine, an article on Natural Tunnel (author unknown) states, "Exploration of the tunnel and the construction of the line of railway through it are described by the late J. H. McCue, the engineer who surveyed and constructed the original line. . . ." The article quotes McCue's description of work in and around the Tunnel but provides no specific reference to the source. McCue's description reads as a firsthand account and will be included later.

It is most unfortunate that, other than those wood engravings referenced earlier, there is only one known photographic image—hopefully, more will turn up—of Natural Tunnel that might provide insight into the task facing the engineer. The January 7, 1888, issue of the *Engineering and Mining Journal* provides a photograph of the North Portal (see Figure 23). A picture of the South Portal, the more grandiose approach to the Tunnel, would provide much greater insight.

It is fortunate that an engineer and excellent writer with a discerning eye for construction visited in 1893, only four to five years after track was laid through the Tunnel. In the May 4, 1893, issue of the *Engineering News,* Emile Low provides not only a description of engineering and construction in the Tunnel, which reads as if he spoke to those with firsthand knowledge, but also a map showing detail of the area, especially as it applies to the railroad (see Figure 24). Using Low as a guide, let us look at the engineering approach to the Tunnel.

THE GREAT NATURAL TUNNEL ON THE SOUTH ATLANTIC & OHIO RAILROAD, VIRGINIA.

Figure 23. This photograph from the January 7, 1888, issue of the *Engineering and Mining Journal* shows the North Portal prior to railroad construction; note the logs and debris in the Stock Creek channel. Comparison of this to later views shows that about half the width of the original streambed is now occupied by railroad ballast. No photographic record of the South Portal prior to railroad construction has yet been found.

A railroad proceeding from Clinchport up the valley of Stock Creek must cross and recross the creek because of the stream's entrenched meanders. If the track followed the course of the creek, the radius of the curves would be too tight. Then, upon approaching the rib of the Amphitheater that juts east, atop which is now the Tunnel Overlook—Emile Low's wonderfully named "Eagle's Nest"—the location engineer must make a choice. Stay on the right (east) side of the creek, which would make a very tight curve in the approach to the South Portal, or cut the rib and approach on the left (west) side of the creek.

Perhaps because of W. W. James's caveat of "don't hurt my tunnel," the location engineer originally took the former approach. This fact was not known until the discovery of Low's article. For years, a cut on the east side of Stock Creek, looking much like an old wagon or logging road, was felt to be just that, but Low notes it on his map as the "original Line on which some work was done," coinciding with this puzzling cut. Grading was started on the east side of Stock Creek but abandoned, likely due to the unwieldy curve that would

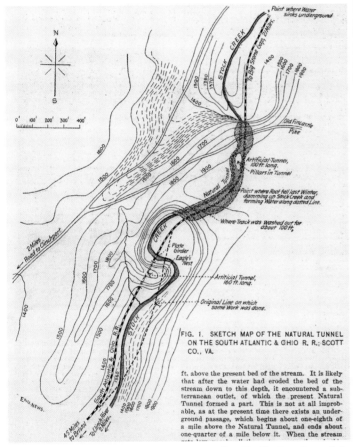

FIG. 1. SKETCH MAP OF THE NATURAL TUNNEL ON THE SOUTH ATLANTIC & OHIO R. R.; SCOTT CO., VA.

ft. above the present bed of the stream. It is likely that after the water had eroded the bed of the stream down to this depth, it encountered a subterranean outlet, of which the present Natural Tunnel formed a part. This is not at all improbable, as at the present time there exists an underground passage, which begins about one-eighth of a mile above the Natural Tunnel, and ends about one-quarter of a mile below it. When the stream

Figure 24. This sketch map accompanies Emile Low's article in the May 4, 1893, issue of the *Engineering News*. Low notes that the original railroad line was to be located east of Stock Creek, and some excavation was done there. The line was moved to the west side of Stock Creek; the plan originally called for the removal of the rib of the Amphitheater jutting east, atop which is the Eagle's Nest, but, thankfully, the excavation was abandoned and the "Little Tunnel" constructed through the rib instead.

result at the South Portal entrance, and the line was moved to the west side.

But an alignment (that is, the ground plan for the railroad bed) on the west side of the creek would require partial removal of the rib, and even then, that alignment would require a reverse curve to enter the South Portal. What to do? Make a tunnel to access the Tunnel!

Low writes, "Just south of the mouth of the Natural Tunnel there is an artificial tunnel [today, this cut is commonly referred to as the "Little Tunnel"], pierced through the point which forms one side of the rotunda like entrance, and mentioned above as the Eagle's Nest. This artificial tunnel is about 160 feet long. The original location obviated this tunnel by merely cutting off the toe of the cliff. Considerable work was done at this point which, of course, destroyed to some extent the natural beauty of the place. Some work was also done on the opposite side of the stream. . . ."

Again, it is unfortunate no photographic record of the South Portal and Amphitheater exists for comparison to a series of photographs that show the line just after completion through the Tunnel (see Figures 25, 26, and 27). These photographs show the near catastrophe that could have occurred, but thankfully, either by an engineering decision, stipulation in the Jameses' right-of-way agreement, or simply the realization by a controlling individual that some things are best left alone, the Eagle's Nest rib, albeit somewhat truncated, was left. Now the railroad had a straight shot at the Tunnel, with no reverse curve.

After piercing the Eagle's Nest rib, a plate girder was laid for the crossing of Stock Creek. On the east side of Stock Creek, a concrete wall—the same wall there today—was constructed for the other

Figure 25. This view is looking north up Stock Creek, probably in late winter, 1890. Note the excavation to the right, which was the original railroad bed, abandoned for the grade shown. The rib of the Amphitheater, atop which is the Eagle's Nest, was partially removed but then abandoned, and the Little Tunnel was excavated. Stock Creek originally flowed to the left, about where the old SA&O wood-burner is sitting, but was forced into its present channel by the railroad bed. (Photograph mounted on linen, courtesy of Robert L. Harvey)

rocks were pulled into the line, and the voids ballasted with gravel.

McCue describes it thusly: "When I made the first survey of this tunnel I found it filled with driftwood and other debris which had almost closed up the opening, although prior to that time the natives had occasionally ridden through it on horseback. On account of the stream of water flowing through it, it was seldom used by pedestrians. It is strange that a natural wonder of such magnitude should have been so little known prior to the time the railroad was built. The natives knew it as "Stock Creek Sink" and did not seem to appreciate the fact that they had in their midst one of the most wonderful pieces of nature's handiwork. . . . [It would seem that McCue either did not speak to the right "native" or spend any time researching the Tunnel's history; these words smack of a condescending outsider's view.]

end of the plate girder. From that point to the Hidden Tunnel (to be discussed later), for a distance of approximately 750 feet, fill material was required to maintain the level of the line some 12 to 15 feet above Stock Creek and the floor of the Tunnel.

Where did this fill material come from? From the Tunnel itself! As stated previously, many visitors to the Tunnel noted the large amount of debris, primarily rocks from roof collapse and falls from the walls, as well as driftwood from floods, choking the Tunnel (see Figures 7, 8, 15-18, and 23). The builders had a ready-made source. After removal of the wood, the

"After the removal of the driftwood and other debris that had been washed into the tunnel at times of excessive high water, it was ascertained that the base was sufficiently wide for both the stream and the railway. The loose rock was then thrown over on one side, forming the foundation for the roadbed. This was raised to proper grade, which left an unobstructed way on the other side of the tunnel for the stream. . . ."

Thus by a fell stroke, in the years 1888-1889, a singularity in the human experience was diminished. Today, the interior of the Tunnel appears

Figure 26. This view, probably late winter, 1890, looks from the mouth of the Little Tunnel to the South Portal. Only minor excavation of the wall occurred here. (Photograph mounted on linen, courtesy of Robert L. Harvey)

dominated by the railroad grade, but before, the visitor would have seen a huge room, nearly an acre underground, with a roof an average of 80 feet above his head. The sense of space and the sense of sheer weight above, though still impressive, must have been so much greater then.

Stock Creek had to change, too. Before the railroad came through the Tunnel, the stream entered the North Portal and made a sharp curve to the left (east), then a curve to the right (west), before sweeping out of the Tunnel along the Amphitheater's west wall to the Eagle's Nest rib. Now it was forced into a straighter, though still curved, line through the Tunnel, along the ballast. Stock Creek, though, would have (and still has) its revenge.

The sharp curve made by the stream after entering the North Portal was too tight for the track to follow. The answer? Again, a tunnel—a "tunnel within a tunnel," if you will. Low describes it this way: ". . . it will be seen that in order to utilize the tunnel for railway purposes, it was necessary to drive a short tunnel through the spur intervening between the two caverns or grottoes. [Low subdivides the Tunnel into two distinct sections, or caverns, one the room formed by Stock Creek at the North Portal before the sharp, left-hand curve, the other the much larger main room.] This tunnel is about 100 ft. long and was driven close to the eastern, or left-hand side. The track of the railway through the Natural Tunnel is generally from 12 to 15 ft. above the original surface. The floor of the artificial tunnel is necessarily of the same elevation. On account of this construction, a large pillar measuring 100 ft. in length and from 25 ft. to 30 ft. in width or thickness, stands near the upper end of the tunnel." Surprisingly, especially from an engineering point of view, he adds, "The removal of this pillar would greatly enhance the grandeur of this natural curiosity."

McCue describes it this way: "At about the center of the tunnel there was found a natural column of limestone projecting from the roof to the base with an aperture on one side sufficiently large to take care of the stream of water. The only blasting done in the construction of the track was in boring through this column a distance of about 16 feet. After this was done a supporting column was left in the center of the tunnel between the railroad track and the stream. There were no projections nor corners to be knocked off."

It can be assumed that McCue was working from a faulty memory, as, indeed, the pillar resulting from the boring is approximately 100 feet long,

Figure 27. View from the mouth of the South Portal to the rib of the Amphitheater and the Little Tunnel. A straight line from the boulder (the site of the present Lower Tunnel Overlook) to the edge of the Amphitheater in the upper right third of the photograph would approximate the original slope. The boulder now lies in at least three pieces, two still at the present Lower Tunnel Overlook, and one in Stock Creek, below. (Photograph mounted on linen, courtesy of Robert L. Harvey)

though the presence of a natural-solution cavity in the column (one exists near stream level now) would explain his figure.

Regardless, the deed—some say the damage—was done. The South Atlantic and Ohio Railroad had laid the track through the Tunnel and, while changing it, had opened it to the world.

SIDE PASSAGES

Local lore has it that, for a short while, until the current moniker became the popular name, the area was called "Double Tunnel," obviously for the Little Tunnel and Natural Tunnel (this name was also used for the area between Big Stone Gap and Appalachia for a time). Given that there are actually three tunnels present, it could have been called "Triple Tunnel."

Some final notes on McCue. While *Trains* magazine seems to imply that McCue was the design engineer for construction at the Tunnel, it should be pointed out that in a deposition for a legal matter involving the Sunbright station, McCue stated that at the time the SA&O was building in the area, he was with the East Tennessee, Virginia & Georgia Railroad. Further, in correspondence regarding grade revisions near Duffield in 1926-1927, C. E. Burchfield, then division superintendent of the Appalachia Division of the Southern Railway, stated that McCue had told him that he proposed a grade for the original SA&O line through the Devil's Racepath. This grade (along the route of present U.S. 23) would have been a gentle 1% but would have required an enormous divestiture of funds for cut-and-fill work on Purchase Ridge, no doubt one of the reasons SA&O management opted for the gentler grades—and lesser cost—of Stock Creek Valley and the Tunnel.

N-492 NATURAL TUNNEL, VIRGINIA.

14 MILES WEST OF GATE CITY, VA. ON U. S. 23   E-5350

N-493 NIGHT-TIME SCENE OF NATURAL TUNNEL, VIRGINIA.

14 MILES WEST OF GATE CITY, VA. ON U. S. 23

N-999 NATURAL TUNNEL, VIRGINIA

14 MILES WEST OF GATE CITY, VA. ON U. S. 23

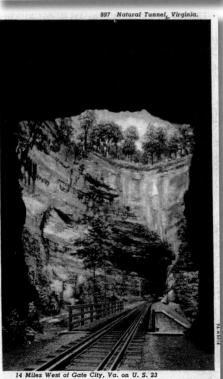

997 *Natural Tunnel, Virginia.*

14 Miles West of Gate City, Va. on U. S. 23

V 735 NATURAL TUNNEL IN SOUTHWESTERN VIRGINIA

45828

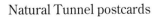

Natural Tunnel postcards

22132 NATURAL TUNNEL, BRISTOL, VA. TENN.

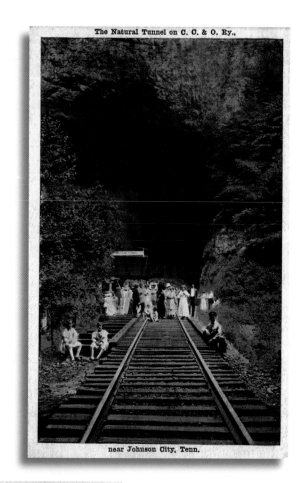

The Natural Tunnel on C. C. & O. Ry.,

near Johnson City, Tenn.

V-900 ENTRANCE BUILDING TO NATURAL TUNNEL, SHOWING LOVER'S LEAP IN THE

BACKGROUND, NATURAL TUNNEL, VA.

Natural Tunnel postcards

508:-NATURAL TUNNEL. IN SOUTHWESTERN VIRGINIA.

33911

Natural Tunnel postcard

Natural Tunnel and Caverns
Corporation stock certificate

View of Rye Cove from Cove Ridge

POOR DOTSON/DODSON/HORTON
THE DANGLING SALTPETER HUNTER

HE WAS BROUGHT TO THE TOP BEFORE THE WYTHE WHOLLY UNTWISTED; BUT THOUGH LIFE WAS PRESERVED, TERROR HAD PRODUCED AN EFFECT SIMILAR TO THAT RECORDED IN OTHER INSTANCES. HIS BUSHY LOCKS WERE BLANCHED "WHITE AS WOOL," AND TO HIS DYING DAY HE BORE A MEMENTO OF HIS NARROW ESCAPE FROM A FEARFUL DEATH.

—W. H. C., 1844

 good story—true or not—develops a life of its own, and one such story is associated with the Tunnel even to this day. Many locals still recount the tale of the dangling saltpeter prospector, with no response to the query of its source other than "somebody told me." Unlike some tales associated with the Tunnel told elsewhere in this book, this one appears plausible, and it is interesting to follow its twists and embellishments through time.

As recounted in Chapter 3, saltpeter prospecting and recovery has been noted both in the Tunnel and nearby caves and solution cavities. Many solution cavities are present in the wall of the Amphitheater, and most appear as small pockets and crevices. But as any good caver will tell you, "you don't know what you got until you look." Certainly at some time in the past—apparently around the War of 1812—someone was having a look, had a wee bit of trouble, and gave us a great story.

In 1844, the author known only as W. H. C. first told the story to a broad audience in "Mountain Scenery of Virginia" in the *Southern Literary Messenger*. Noting a "certain vein of saltpeter," our prospector was determined to have a look, but for want of a suitable rope, then "scarce and costly articles," one was fashioned from "green hickory wythes." His companions lowered him some "one hundred and fifty feet below the top of the precipice," over an overhang (perhaps at the South Portal entrance), and were thus unable to see him at his task.

The prospector crawled into the opening to "throw the nitrous earth to the bottom of the rock," finished, and then signaled for his comrades to pull him up. On his ascent, he looked up, only to see his rope untwisting. Struck dumbfounded, he could not yell to his friends and abandoned himself to his fate. Fortunately, and like all classic good tales, just in the nick of time, he was pulled over the brink, where he collapsed, and his friends found that his "bushy locks" had turned completely white.

Not one to leave any good story unstolen, in 1845 Henry Howe took it and added some embellishments. Howe seems to have placed the perilous descent/ascent in the neighborhood of Lover's Leap (though an engraving appears to show the near mishap at the South Portal, see Figure 28), and this time our hero has a name—Dotson. In Howe's version, he does have a rope, but alas, "not being sufficiently long, the last length, which was tied around his waist, was made of the bark of leatherwood."

When lowered from the top, Dotson "was still horizontally distant twelve or fourteen feet, being so thrown by the overhanging of the rock above." This distance, of course, made it difficult for him to reach the crevice (something which W. H. C. does not address). But Dotson had a pole with a hook, and as he pulled himself to the crevice, the hook slipped, and off he swung. Now nothing more than a human pendulum, his oscillations became so wild that a friend on the opposite wall of the Amphitheater "instinctively drew back, for it appeared as if he [Dotson] was slung at him across the abyss."

Dotson then became very busy preventing himself "from being dashed against the rock" time and again. Eventually, though, the pendulum wound down.

But just as he thought himself safe, Dotson heard a crack above his head, and looking up, "he saw the strands of the bark rope breaking." Our hero grasped the bark rope above the break and shouted, "Pull! For God's sake, pull!" and he was hauled over the top by his friends, where he promptly fainted.

One would think that enough is enough, but Howe's Dotson—who apparently kept his original hair color—replaced the bark rope section with one of hemp, and did it all again. Unfortunately, "His

Lower Entrance to the Natural Tunnel.

Figure 28. This engraving, from Henry Howe's 1845 *Historical Collections of Virginia,* shows Dotson prior to the slipping of the hook, the snapping of the leatherwood, and the entreaty of "Pull! For God's sake, pull!"

only reward was the gratification of his curiosity. The hole extended but a few feet."

The Reverend C. Collins recounted Howe's Dotson story in 1855 in the *Ladies Repository,* "taking the liberty to correct his figures." The Reverend Collins moves the enterprise back to W. H. C.'s South Portal and overhang, to "a cave about halfway up" (one which I have never seen), or about 200 feet below the "precipice . . . here about four hundred and ten feet in hight [sic]."

We must forgive the preacher if he has misplaced the tale, as he writes, "Our impressions of this lovely spot are the reminiscences of thirteen years ago," which, interestingly, is about the time W. H. C. wrote. We must also thank the Reverend Collins, as he continued the theme of Natural Tunnel versus Natural Bridge by comparing our Dotson to the Natural Bridge's Colonel Piper, who carved "his way up the perpendicular walls of that awful chasm with his knife," and after his friends pulled him over the top with a rope, fainted as his hair turned white.

In 1857, *Harper's New Monthly Magazine* published the story "A Winter in the South," supposedly by a Mr. Broadacre but actually by David Hunter Strother, telling the fanciful tale of the Broadacres and their companions' journeys. Here Dotson is given a first name—George—and his adventures are much less dangerous. True, he does swing pendulum-like in his saltpeter pursuit, but neither his hair nor his rope suffer any consequence.

R. L. Bachman continued the saga in 1870 in the *Hamilton Literary Magazine.* Our hero is again unnamed, and again, he descends on a rope with a section of leatherwood bark, and he again goes "swinging, swinging, pendulum like, over the terrible chasm below." This time, however, the leatherwood begins snapping during the swings, and he grasps above the breaks and is pulled to safety by his companions before the end of the oscillations, with no mention of hair or consciousness affected. But, like Dotson, "he re-adjusted his rope and a second time went down, "only to be disappointed as all the rest.

Just when you would think no more twists to the tale could be told, Edward A. Pollard upped the ante. In his 1871 book *The Virginia Tourist,* he starts the tale in same fashion as his predeces-

sors, only giving the subject the name "Dodson." Dodson, too, suffers the too-short rope, supplanted by leatherwood plaits. He hangs too far away and uses the pole, only to have the hook slip, with the resultant oscillations. In this version, however, "an eagle, scared from its nest in the fissure and excited to protect it, flew out and attacked the already alarmed adventurer."

Pulling his pocketknife to defend himself and stabbing at the eagle, "he severed one of the strands of his bark rope." This time his voice does not leave him, and his screams of "Pull! For God's sake, pull!" are answered. While there is no report on his hair, he does faint. This time there is no second trip down.

Charles B. Coale, in his 1878 book *The Life and Adventures of Wilburn Waters,* devotes a chapter to "The Natural Bridge of Scott" but spends most of his words on the human-pendulum story. Coale names our hero "Horton" (a common name in the immediate area), and the same misfortunes befall our man at the end of the rope—minus the eagle attack.

Coale's retelling has a bit more realistic conclusion. Coale states that, when recovered over the precipice, "Horton, it is said, was about as near dead as alive when he reached the top, and was no doubt a wise if not better man after that, and never again hunted 'Peter dirt' in that direction."

The moral of the story would seem to be this: A good Virginia lad, if he hopes to keep his hair color, should stick to flat ground. A hemp rope of sufficient length is better than a short one with leatherwood or hickory wythe additions. And lastly, following the example of Uncle Ike, be lowered down, not pulled back up.

Side Rope

The April 18, 1928, issue of the *Nashua* (Iowa) *Reporter* adds an interesting twist to the tale of Poor Dotson (one wonders if the newly organized Natural Tunnel and Caverns Corporation was beginning to dabble in promotion). Its version of the story places a man over the side of the Amphitheater—in a box suspended by two ropes—in search of gold buried in a cave, left there by "white men pursued by Indians."

Again an eagle attacks, and again our hero is careless with his knife, but one rope holds, by which he is pulled up. Instead of blanching, "he was found to be demented as a result of the terrifying experience," and the paper claims to that day of the existence of a "goblin, deranging the minds of marauders seeking treasure . . . far up in the Blue Ridge mountains of Virginia. . . ." The paper also warns readers to beware of the spirit of the Indian princess that inhabits the Tunnel, a suicide victim after her father, a Mingo—an Ohio Valley tribe!—chief refused her betrothal to "Cochesa."

A RAILROAD RUNS THROUGH IT
RAILROADING AND THE NATURAL TUNNEL, 1890-1939

AND NOW WE APPROACH A WONDER OF THE WIL-
DERNESS, WHICH, THOUGH LONG KNOWN TO GEOL-
OGISTS AND OCCASIONAL TRAVELERS, HAS AS YET
GAINED BUT LITTLE ATTENTION FROM THE BUSY OUT-
SIDE WORLD WHICH IS PRONE TO TAKE ITS MARVELS
AS A MATTER OF COURSE, AND TROUBLES ITSELF TO
GO AND LOOK AT THEM ONLY WHEN THE ROYAL ROAD
OF THE STEEL RAIL HAS MADE IT EASY TO DO SO.
—SOUTH ATLANTIC AND OHIO RAILROAD
PROMOTIONAL BOOK, 1890

SPECIAL POLICEMAN WILL BE ALONG AND GOOD
ORDER IS GUARANTEED.
—SPECIAL EXCURSION PROMOTIONAL FLYER,
AUGUST 20, 1904

y early 1890, the South Atlantic and Ohio had reached Big Stone Gap, and by August, regular passenger service to Bristol was occurring (see Figures 29, 30, and 31). On June 10, 1890, the first train of coal arrived in Bristol from Big Stone Gap. While the coal drove the construction and is still the only reason the line exists today, the passenger traffic is by far the more interesting. One could now ride to—and through—the Tunnel.

In 1890, the SA&O published a book touting the scenic beauty and wealth of natural resources (coal, iron ore, timber, and "marble," the latter actually a coarse-grained, reddish limestone suitable as decorative stone) along the route, plus the communities "sure" to grow to cities now that the railroad had opened the way, including the end of the line (at that time), Big Stone Gap. It is important to remember that, at this time, the SA&O was owned by the Virginia, Tennessee & Carolina Steel & Iron Company, which had a vested interest in promoting development of the area. The book describes at length the Tunnel, not only because of its uniqueness, but also because of the role the company intended it to play in their enterprise.

From the book: "This remarkable, and from an engineering standpoint, highly advantageous work of Dame Nature, is now owned, with much contiguous land, by the Virginia, Tennessee & Carolina Steel & Iron Company, who propose to greatly improve the surroundings and create in this picturesque region a new and unique resort for that large element, the touring class. The tunnel will be illuminated by electricity.

"When it is remembered that this place is but nine

Figure 29. The first train to make it through Natural Tunnel and to Big Stone Gap, probably May 1890. This old SA&O diamond-stack woodburner was photographed near present Oakview Cemetery in Big Stone Gap. The patch of white sandstone at the crest of Stone Mountain at upper left is still visible today. (Photograph courtesy of Kenny Fannon)

hours from Natural Bridge, seven hours from Roanoke, and within a brief ride from the great through route between the cities of the North, and Knoxville, Chattanooga, Atlanta, and the whole Southwest [*Note:* Again the comparison with Natural Bridge, and the times of travel seem a bit shortened, even by today's standards], it is safe to predict that the annual visitation, as soon as the proper preparations are made for safety and comfort, will be very large."

To support its assertions on the beauty and resources of the area, the book is profusely illustrated with engravings. The Tunnel interior and exterior are both shown (see Figures 32-35). The SA&O had entered the tourist trade.

By 1891, the SA&O was playing on its use of the Tunnel for passage through Purchase Ridge. Its timetables proudly proclaim "The Natural Tunnel Route" (see Figure 36). Until 1924, the Tunnel was listed in the timetables for the line (both the Virginia and Southwestern, and the Southern), but not as a station stop. It the early days, trains would pause to allow visitors to gawk from the cars and sometimes alight for a moment for a better look.

Someone wanting to spend a little more time than a quick look-see could also depart the train at the Natural Tunnel Depot, walk to the Tunnel, and catch the train on its return trip. The listing "Natural Tunnel" in the SA&O timetable appears to actually refer to the depot at Glenita. There is no evidence a depot, per se, existed at the Tunnel, and certainly it would be a poor location for freight or passengers, with no direct road access.

Recall that W. W. James's right-of-way deed required the railroad to construct a depot "on the tract of land conveyed to it by William P. Good." Though the record is incomplete on the subject, it appears Mr. Good's property was located entirely south of the Tunnel along Stock Creek. By the 1930s, the Glenita Depot was located here, and it is assumed that was the location, also, during the early railroad days.

Also, recall that James's deed specified that the railroad would construct "a platform . . . at such convenient points across the mouth of said tunnel as may be designated by the parties of the first part." This platform was part of James's plan to make the Tunnel a tourist attraction, but he sold out, and the requirement did not need to be fulfilled. Visitors to the Tunnel had to make do with a blanket on the ground (see Figures 37-39). This situation would change, but first—of course—there would be another railroad upheaval.

Dr. John Bailey had been fired before the railroad even made it to Natural Tunnel. Immediately asserting that he was due a large sum for his services as general manager of the SA&O and president of the construction company building the line, Bailey entered litigation in an attempt to wrest control of the railroad from the VT&CS&IC.

Bailey's adversary in the struggle was John C. Haskell, who had succeeded Bailey after a short series of different individuals as manager of the line. Haskell was a one-armed, ex-Confederate colonel who had served under General Daniel Harvey Hill in North Carolina and later lost his arm at the Battle of Gaines's Mill on June 27, 1862, refusing chloroform for his surgery. The papers of the time referred to him as a "gallant Civil War hero," and by all accounts he was a tough opponent.

From 1890 to 1896—depending on who was suing

Figure 30. SA&O Engine Number 2 poses on the tracks, likely near the community of Glenita, circa 1890. (Photograph courtesy of Kenny Fannon)

whom in which court—Bailey was reinstated a number of times, only later to be replaced by Haskell. At times, a train would leave Bristol under the direction of one gentleman, only to have the entire crew replaced by another before they got to Appalachia, because the court had ruled in favor of the other that day! There are humorous stories of the replacement crew collecting fares from the previous crew for passage home. Other stories tell about the practice of hiding equipment and supplies, even running engines onto side tracks and pulling the line up behind them, in case "the other guy is boss tomorrow." The crews, loyal to their leader, Haskell or Bailey, took to carrying arms.

As the question goes, "Is this any way to run a railroad?" Obviously not. In 1892, the Central Trust Company of New York, the mortgage holder for the companies, filed suit alleging their insolvency. Judge Bond of the Circuit Court of the U.S. Western Dis-

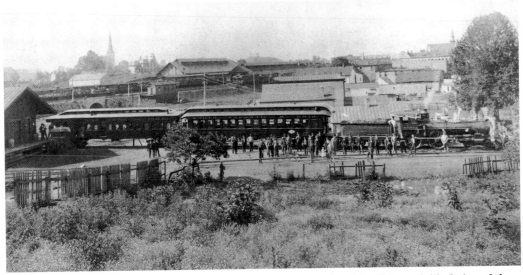

Figure 31. This SA&O train, in the Bristol yard, is bannered and beribboned, likely in celebration of the start of regular passenger service between Bristol and Big Stone Gap, then the end of the line, in August of 1890. (Photograph courtesy of Kenny Fannon)

the VT&CS&IC) had voluntarily asked to be appointed receivers, thus bypassing the question of jurisdiction. So, the situation stood, but the damage was done.

After a few more court proceedings, Bailey finally settled for a cash payment, but the railroad and its parent company were ordered sold by decree of the District Court dated July 30, 1896. Bailey, at the age of 47, died the following year. Needless to say, with all this trouble, the SA&O did not follow through on any improvements at the Tunnel, and no tourism infrastructure was built. Another hundred years would pass before the Tunnel was electrified.

On April 28, 1898, Receiver Haskell sold the SA&O to Messrs. B. S. Clarke and Marshall Clyde, who represented a committee of the mortgage holders. Haskell remained as manager of the line. It is unclear if the deal, which included a cash down payment with the balance due within six months, was ever consummated, because on January 27, 1899, the railroad was sold to what the papers of the time called the "George Carter Syndicate."

George L. Carter was an enigmatic figure—he refused interviews and attempts at biographies—and a huge player in the mineral and land development of Virginia, West Virginia, North Carolina, and Kentucky. Before he died in 1936, he left in his

trict of Virginia found for the plaintiff and ordered a receiver appointed. Haskell was appointed receiver for the SA&O.

Bailey jumped on the bandwagon and instantly filed another suit, alleging he was the rightful receiver. Stockholders of the VT&CS&IC filed suit against the company. Bailey and the stockholders then joined forces and filed a petition for reconsideration of the judge's order. The judge's order was overturned, and the bill of complaint—that the court could not hear a case in Virginia involving a New York-based company (New York Trust) and a New Jersey company (the railroad and the VT&CS&IC)—was upheld. In other words, a real legal mess.

In 1894, the case went before the United States Supreme Court. The Court, Justice Shiras writing, found that the Western District Circuit Court had not erred, because Haskell (and D. H. Conklin for wake, either directly or by development and then sale, the Virginia Iron, Coal and Coke Company (VICCC), Pittston Coal Company, the Virginia Pocahontas Company, the Carolina, Clinchfield & Ohio Railroad (CC&O), the coal town of Coalwood, West Virginia, and many, many other concerns.

At the time of his purchase of the SA&O, Carter was attempting to put the iron-ore, coal, coke, timber, and other resources, along with the railroads of the region, under one roof. To this end, under the auspices of the existing VICCC, he bought up, over time, essentially all of the properties of the VT&CS&IC and created a new railroad, chartered January 19, 1899, by act of the Virginia General Assembly. This new railroad would combine the Bristol, Elizabethton & North Carolina Railroad, serving the timber and iron-ore deposits of that area, and the SA&O, serving the coalfields and coke ovens of Lee and Wise counties, into the Virginia & Southwestern Railway (V&SW).

The V&SW, like its predecessor, made use of its

THE GREAT NATURAL TUNNEL.
1. Looking in the Eastern Entrance.
2. A Glimpse of the Amphitheater from Eastern Entrance.
3. Western Entrance.
4. Artificial Tunnel at Eastern Entrance.

EASTERN ENTRANCE TO THE BIG TUNNEL AND GENERAL VIEW OF AMPHITHEATER.

Figure 32. This wood engraving, from an 1890 SA&O promotional book, shows the southern approach to the Tunnel. The Amphitheater has been stretched in this view. Compare this view to Figure 25.

Figure 33. These four views are from an 1890 SA&O promotional book. View 2 seems to show a small building near the South Portal entrance, perhaps a supply shack, but the Pavilion was not in place at this time. View 3 implies that Stock Creek is a river. Compare View 4 to Figure 27, especially the two stumps in the foreground and the boulder at the present Lower Tunnel Overlook.

THE NATURAL TUNNEL LOOKING EAST.

Figure 34. This wood engraving is from an 1890 SA&O promotional book and is a view out of the South Portal. Note that the small shack seen in the previous figure is not shown.

THE NATURAL TUNNEL, LOOKING WEST.

Figure 35. This wood engraving is from an 1890 SA&O promotional book. The artist has tried to show both the natural Stock Creek entrance and the Hidden Tunnel in one view; the entirety of both cannot be seen from any one point in the Tunnel.

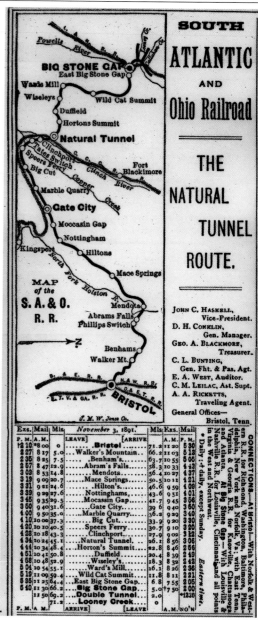

Figure 36. This November 3, 1891, SA&O time-table proudly proclaims "The Natural Tunnel Route." John C. Haskell was firmly in control of the line at this time. (Timetable from the John Dale collection)

Figure 38. The Loyal Order of Odd Fellows, replete with band, posed at the North Portal, circa 1900. Large groups appear to have preferred the North Portal because it had more space. (Photograph courtesy of Richard Whitt)

Figure 37. This photograph, circa 1905-1906, shows a picnic outing with entertainment at the South Portal. Before construction of the Pavilion, visitors had to make do with a blanket on the ground, or, as in this case, an old railroad tie. The gentleman standing in the center is Elbert H. Walker; in a couple of years, he would own the Tunnel. Note that Mr. Walker appears to be "packing a piece" in his waistband. The bottle in the wicker basket is likely payment for the banjo player and fiddler. (Photograph donated to Natural Tunnel State Park by Dave Walker, grandson of Elbert H. Walker)

Figure 39. An unknown group posed at the North Portal, exact date uncertain, circa 1890-1910. This photograph, of unknown origin, is labeled in the Natural Tunnel State Park files as "Theodore Roosevelt and Party." It is my opinion that the photograph shows a special excursion train outing. See further discussion in Chapter 14.

unique passage through Purchase Ridge. It proudly proclaimed the Tunnel in timetables (see Figure 40) and letterhead (see Figure 41). Newer, more powerful engines were put on the line (see Figure 42). The movement of coal over the line increased with the growing output of the Southwest Virginia coalfields (see Figure 43).

But, oh, those railroad rogues! By 1901, the VICCC and the V&SW were in receivership, and Carter had moved on. The line operated under receivership until September 14, 1906, when the Southern Railway bought the entire capital stock of the V&SW. The line operated semi-autonomously (but with new management) until July 21, 1916, when it was absorbed into the Southern Railway and operated as the Appalachia Division.

One would think in all these wheelings and dealings that the Tunnel property would end up in the hands of Carter, but that was not the case, probably because Carter saw no mineral value, meaning coal and iron ore, in the property, and he certainly wasn't interested in the tourist trade. Carter's principal area of interest in the old VT&CS&IC property was eastern Wise and Dickenson counties, where his new railroad would run. The western Wise and Lee county properties were bought up by the Interstate Coal & Iron Company, chartered May 25, 1899. This company was composed of former stockholders, principally New York capitalists, of the VT&CS&IC. They would hold the lease to Natural Tunnel until its sale to Elbert H. Walker on December 15, 1908.

As evinced by old postcards (see Figure 44), at least by 1906, a pavilion (see Figures 45 and 46) had been built at the South Portal of the Tunnel. It is unclear who built this structure, but it appears

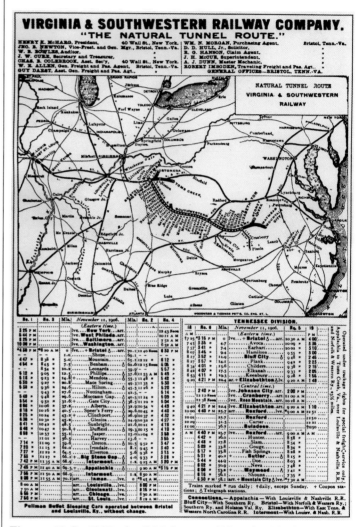

Figure 40. In 1899, the SA&O consolidated with the Bristol, Elizabethton & North Carolina Railroad to form the Virginia & Southwestern. Like its predecessor, the V&SW was proud to claim "The Natural Tunnel Route." Note that this November 11, 1906, timetable lists J. H. McCue, who claimed credit for building the track through Natural Tunnel, as superintendent. Only two months prior, the Southern Railway had bought the entire capital stock of the V&SW, though the line operated under its own name until 1916. (Timetable courtesy of Robert L. Harvey)

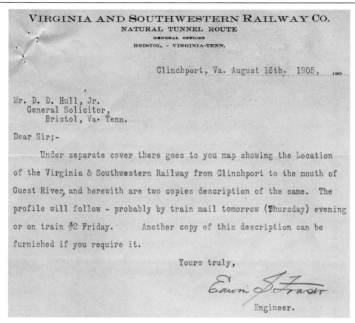

Figure 41. An August 16, 1905, letter from engineer E. Fraser to V&SW General Solicitor D. D. Hull, Jr., with "Natural Tunnel Route" letterhead. The letter appears to discuss the planned—but doomed—route up the Clinch River Valley. (Courtesy of Kenny Fannon)

Figure 42. This V&SW engine had run the Tunnel and was waiting to "make up train" near Appalachia, circa 1910. (Courtesy of Kenny Fannon)

NATURAL TUNNEL, V. & S. W. RY.

THIS Tunnel is 75 feet high at the East entrance, and is 900 feet long, the railroad making a complete reverse curve inside the tunnel. A large Creek flows through the tunnel and no excavating was necessary to enable the railway to build through.

It is 364 feet from Track to Top of Rock Ledge.

OUR COAL ALL COMES THROUGH THIS TUNNEL. THAT ISN'T A GOOD REASON WHY YOU SHOULD BUY IT, BUT THERE **ARE** SOME EXCELLENT REASONS. WON'T YOU LET US SHOW YOU? A CARD WILL BRING OUR REPRESENTATIVE.

Virginia Bituminous Coal Co.
Bristol, Va. - Tenn.

Figure 43. The Virginia Bituminous Coal Company used the Tunnel as a selling point for its commodity, as seen in this flyer, circa 1910. (Courtesy of Gil Bledsoe)

OBSERVATION CAR TRAIN
ENTERING NATURAL TUNNEL
SOUTHWEST VIRGINIA

Figure 44. An observation car with passengers stops to take the view at the South Portal and pose for a photograph, from which this hand-tinted postcard was made, circa 1910-1915.

Figure 45. A view of the Pavilion at the South Portal, as seen from the present Lower Tunnel Overlook. The V&SW probably built the Pavilion circa 1906. This photograph is included in the January 1944 issue of *Trains* magazine. The source of the photograph is not stated, and the Pavilion was long gone by then.

Figure 46. The Pavilion as seen from the mouth of the South Portal, from the January 1944 issue of *Trains* magazine.

most likely that the V&SW did, because the railroad was actively promoting special excursions to the Tunnel (see Figure 47). Until the Pavilion was in place, activity around the Tunnel appears to have occurred mainly at the North Portal, where the creek bottom and adjacent hillsides allowed a little room. But with the Pavilion, the South Portal became the party place and center for dances and galas (see Figure 48). Excursionists and travelers sent postcards home showing the festivities and views of the Tunnel (see Figures 49 and 50).

In these early tourist years, Natural Tunnel had a bit of a risqué reputation and apparently attracted rowdy crowds. The "refreshments on the train and at the Tunnel" also included demijohns of the more potent variety, distilled in the surrounding hills and hollows, albeit they were supplied by some of the passengers. Around 1905 or 1906, the V&SW had contracted J. D. Broadwater to be the railroad's special agent, and he may well have been one of the special policemen who would "be along and good order is guaranteed."

When Prohibition was declared in 1920, it seems as though these spirituous liquids could still be obtained in the area—local lore tells that Natural

Tunnel Caverns served as a speakeasy—but for the most part, visitors by railroad came to see the Tunnel and not to purchase bathtub gin.

Special excursion trains continued at least into

MOONLIGHT EXCURSION

To Natural Tunnel, Aug. 20, 1904.

On the night of August 20th a Moonlight excusion will be run over the V. & S.W. from Inman to the Natural Tunnel and return at the following very low rate for the round trip:

INMAN,	$1.00	ORETON,	.65
APPALACHIA,	1.00	JASPER,	.50
INTERMONT,	1.00	DUFFIELD,	.30
BIG STONE GAP,	1.00	NORA,	.20
ELVERTON,	1.00		

This excursion is for white people only. Train leaves Inman at 8 p.m., arriving at the Tunnel at about 9:30. Returning train leaves Tunnel at 2 a.m. This train will connection with the train from Stonega both going and returning. Going excursion will leave Appalachia on arrival of L. & N. train from Norton.

The Tunnel will be well lighted and everyone is assured a good time. Plenty of free music and dancing. Special policeman will be along and good order is guaranteed.

Refreshments on the train and at the Tunnel.

Don't fail to go and enjoy the most pleasant excursion of the season.

Capt. R.J. GRUBB,
C. P. SPROLES

Figure 47. This flyer promotes a special excursion train by the V&SW to the Tunnel. Captain R. J. Grubb was the conductor on the first SA&O passenger train to Big Stone Gap and was obviously still working for the V&SW. Can you spot the typographical errors in the announcement? (From the files of Natural Tunnel State Park)

Figure 49. This hand-tinted postcard, circa 1910, shows a large party at the Pavilion. Postcards from this time period variously refer to the Tunnel being near Gate City, Bristol, Big Stone Gap, or simply the Virginia-Tennessee line. (From the files of Natural Tunnel State Park)

Figure 48. It's party time, circa 1910. Once in place, the Pavilion became the center of activity for visits to the Tunnel. With the area covered in soot from steam engines, these ladies must have had some difficulty keeping their white linen dresses clean. (Courtesy of Kenny Fannon)

Figure 50. What's wrong with this picture? Of all Natural Tunnel postcards, this is probably the most collectible, because it's a mistake! Note that the publisher puts the Tunnel on the CC&O line instead of the V&SW.

Southern Railway continued to provide passenger service from Bristol to Appalachia and St. Charles until 1939. In the early Southern Railway era, as many as four passenger trains a day operated through the Tunnel. On February 28, 1932, the schedule was cut to two a day; the trains were referred to locally as the "Long Dog" (the morning train, freight and passengers) and the "Short Dog" (evening train, predominantly passengers). After 1924, Southern no longer used the appellation "The Natural Tunnel Route," though passenger timetables made prominent note of passage through the Tunnel (see Figure 52).

On May 6, 1939, the last regular passenger train roared through Natural Tunnel on its way home to Bristol. This was the last run of the famed "Lonesome Pine Special" (see Figure 53), the name the one-a-day train had carried for the past several years. From then until now, only train crews or occasional railroad buffs passing through on a special excursion (see Figure 54) could experience the Tunnel from the iron horse. From 1939 until 1982, under the Southern (see Figure 55), and from 1982 until present, under the Norfolk Southern (see Figure 56), the Tunnel served, and serves, as a gateway for the line's lifeblood—coal.

SIDE TRACKS

The Revenge of the Tunnel. The V&SW Timetable No. 15, dated November 11, 1906, has two special instructions regarding train operations in and around Natural Tunnel. Special instruction a-6 states, "Trains must not exceed a speed of eight (8) miles per hour through the corporate limits of Bristol, over Trestle No. 66.6 between Mile-post 66 and 67 and through the Natural Tunnel. . . .

755 TRAIN LEAVING NATURAL TUNNEL, SOUTHWEST VIRGINIA

Figure 51. A postcard home: "Having a wonderful time, wish you were here." This card, from the 1930s, is a linen reproduction of an earlier V&SW card showing a train at the North Portal.

the early Southern Railway era, but by the late 1920s this practice had stopped, probably due to both unprofitability and a lack of adequate space to serve large parties. By 1930, when the Tunnel property was firmly in corporate hands, the Pavilion was gone.

TABLE 53	BRISTOL, APPALACHIA AND ST. CHARLES (Appalachia Division.)		
1 Daily (ET) Eastern Time	Miles	(ET) Eastern Time (CT) Central Time	4 Daily
5 15	.0	Lv Bristol (ET) Ar Va.–Tenn.	12 55
4 15	.0	Bristol (CT) "	11 55
f4 31	5.6	Haskell .... Va	f11 33
4 37	8.1	Benham .... "	11 26
f4 43	10.8	Leonard .... "	f11 19
f4 49	13.1	Phillip .... "	f11 13
4 56	15.4	Mendota .... "	11 07
f	18.0	Silica .... "	f
f5 06	21.4	Mace Springs .... "	f10 56
5 12	25.2	Hilton .... "	10 49
5 22	30.6	Moccasin Gap .... "	10 40
5 27	32.2	Gate City .... "	10 35
f5 36	36.8	Daniboone Yard .... "	f10 22
5 48	40.8	Speer's Ferry .... "	10 12
5 53	43.6	Clinchport .... "	10 07
5 57	45.6	Glenita .... "	10 02
	48.9	Natural Tunnel (See Note)	
6 05	48.9	Sunbright .... "	9 55
6 10	51.4	Duffield .... "	9 51
f	55.5	Jasper .... "	f
f	57.1	Harvey .... "	f
f6 26	60.2	Oreton .... "	f9 38
6 35	65.1	Elverton .... "	9 28
6 41	66.5	Big Stone Gap .... "	9 25
6 50	69.5	Appalachia (So. Ry.) .... "	9 20
7 00	70.1	Appalachia (U. S.) .... Va.	9 15
7 05	69.5	Appalachia (So. Ry.).. Va.	9 05
7 12	71.1	Imboden .... "	8 58
f7 20	74.3	Crest .... "	f8 50
7 25	76.2	Keokee .... "	8 46
f7 35	80.1	Bundy .... "	f8 38
f7 42	82.3	Delvale .... "	f8 33
f7 50	85.9	Purcell .... "	f8 25
7 53	89.1	Pocket .... "	8 18
8 10	91.9	Ar St. Charles Lv	8 10

Trains operate through Natural Tunnel (788 feet long, 120 feet wide, 90 feet high.)
Nottingham is flag stop for Nos. 1 and 4.   f–Flag stop.

Figure 52. In 1916, the old V&SW was finally absorbed into the Southern Railway as the Appalachia Division. The railroad no longer promoted the Tunnel nor called itself "The Natural Tunnel Route." This timetable, probably from the 1930s, simply lists the fact that the line passes through the Tunnel and gives the Tunnel's size. (Timetable from the John Dale collection)

Figure 53. The Lonesome Pine Special, so-named because it traversed that region of Southwest Virginia identified with John Fox, Jr.'s book *The Trail of the Lonesome Pine,* made its last passenger run through the Tunnel on May 6, 1939. From then on, Southern operated the line primarily as a coal road. (Courtesy of Kenny Fannon)

Figure 54. The Southern 4501 steam engine, with a little help from a Norfolk Southern diesel grandson, pulls a special excursion train out of the South Portal, May 1993. I was happily peering out of a coach window at the interior of the Tunnel, my foot propped on an adjacent seat, having cut my right big toe off with a shovel the day before. Some events, anticipated—and paid for—for some time, are worth a little discomfort. (From the files of Natural Tunnel State Park)

Figure 55. After World War II, the railroads made the change from steam to diesel power. Here the January 1948 cover of *Ties* magazine shows Southern Engine 4172 pulling a load of Southwest Virginia coal out of the South Portal.

Figure 56. In 1982, Norfolk and Western merged with Southern to form Norfolk Southern. Southern green was replaced by Norfolk Southern basic Thoroughbred black. Here, Engine 6664 and a helper pull empties out of the North Portal, bound for Appalachia and another load of coal. (From the files of Natural Tunnel State Park)

All trains will approach the Natural Tunnel under full control, expecting to find the track obstructed and will flag through if no signal received from the watchman." There was good reason for this speed limitation, learned, but not always remembered, from tragic experience.

Natural Tunnel is often noted as the easiest railroad route—meaning only minor modification was needed, hence cheap—through Purchase Ridge, but by no means is it the best. No sooner than the SA&O was completed, Stock Creek, often referred to in early descriptions as a small mountain stream or a babbling and murmuring brook, reminded the audacious railroad builders that it was, indeed, a headwaters stream in mountainous terrain.

Stock Creek jumped its banks during a flood in

February of 1893 and promptly washed out a hundred feet of track in the Tunnel, essentially shutting down the line. This situation would happen again and again over the years (even during the writing of this book in late winter of 2002), causing the railroad to raise the roadbed and construct retaining walls. The narrowing of the stream channel due to railbed ballasting, combined with the narrow northern portal entrance and the near-right-angle turn in the creek bed, is a perfect formula for flooding at high flow.

The Tunnel itself would remind the railroad that nature bats last. The January 5, 1893, edition of the *Big Stone Gap Post* notes, "Yesterday's SA&O train, due here at 5:20, was delayed on account of a large stone falling from the dome of Natural Tunnel across the track. The stone was about fifteen feet long by ten wide and it was not a small job clearing and repairing the track. . . ."

The railroad also apparently employed scalers over the years, especially in the early days, to clean debris from the Amphitheater walls and the North Portal. Small stones on the park's present boardwalk at the South Portal still remind the visitor, especially during thaw in late winter, that a 350-foot-high cliff looms overhead.

Lastly, as any good railroader will tell you, the only good curve is no curve, and for the railroad to run the Tunnel, it must follow the curve present there, even with the excavation of the Hidden Tunnel. Early trains often jumped the tracks, spilling their freight, but perhaps the worse disaster happened on Christmas Eve of 1911. A V&SW double-header freight train, speeding into the North Portal, jumped the tracks, either due to excessive speed on the curve or a rock on the track, or perhaps both.

Engineer W. S. Adams and fireman Leland Glover were killed outright, crushed under the debris; fireman J. R. C. Sproles drowned in Stock Creek, held underwater by the wreckage.

Guarding the Tunnel in the War to End All Wars. As part of the war effort during World War I, the federal government took over control of the American railroad system. Wise County maintained a company of the National Guard (known as Company H of the Second Virginia Regiment), headquartered at Big Stone Gap, with the Honorable J. F. Bullitt serving as captain. When the United States entered the war, Company H was recruited to full strength.

Before leaving for training, the company was ordered out to guard the railroads at several important points, including Natural Tunnel, to ensure the flow of coal. Mrs. Ruby Stewart, granddaughter of E. H. Walker, recalled walking the Tunnel and nearby railroad trestles as a young teenager and seeing sandbag barricades, some with soldiers' initials, used either as gun emplacements or shelters. There is no report the Kaiser's minions attempted to attack the Tunnel.

The owners of the V&SW, too, saw the wealth to be made in accessing the eastern Wise and Dickenson county coalfields, and planned a line, to be called the Virginia & Southeastern, all the way to the Breaks on the Russell Fork of the Big Sandy River on the Virginia/Kentucky border—putting the company into direct competition with George L. Carter.

They, of course, lost the race, but as an interesting aside, they developed a secret code, such as the Union Pacific and Central Pacific did during the transcontinental race, by which company personnel could communicate without giving away their plans. Each person within the company and each geographic point of interest was given a name, as were common phrases and actions. Thus, the message "D. D. Hull, Jr., to J. H. McCue: Send seven cars to Appalachia, return with coal to Bristol Engine 101" would be sent as this: "Quinine quinker quadruped quietly quaffing qualm quash quibbling"!

The company went so far as to do surveying, some excavation, and right-of-way purchase up the valley of the Clinch. One poignant note of a would-be seller (circa 1905) in the files of that lost company is worthy of report:

Clinchport Va   RFD #1
Mr. D. D. Hull   Bristol, Va

Dear Sir as you are one of the Virginia & Southeastern Rail Road Co I have a Piece of Land i wold like to sell you or or some of the Co the Land has some Timber & Irne Ore on it & I am a Poore sick Person & hard run to support my self. I am so afflicted & so frightful i fear the nois of the Trains will cause my death if I dount move Further from the Road I am not able to have a House built & i sincerely hop you will take Pity on me & Buy my Piece of Land. Please let me here from you at once

Martha Carter

THE CAVE OF THE UNKNOWN
SUBTERRANE ASSOCIATED WITH NATURAL TUNNEL

WE REPEAT THAT OUR EXPLORATION COULD ONLY BE PARTIAL, AS THE EXTENT OF THE CAVE IS AS YET UNKNOWN, AND SO LITTLE HAS THE CURIOSITY OF THE NEIGHBORS BEEN TAXED WITH THIS NATURAL WONDER THAT IT IS YET WITHOUT A NAME, EXCEPT THAT WHICH OUR PARTY AGREED TO BESTOW UPON IT—THE "CAVE OF THE UNKNOWN."

—EDWARD A. POLLARD, 1871

he cave Pollard mentions above now has a name: Bolling Cave. More rightly, Bowling Cave, but more rightly still, Bowlin Cave.

For many visitors to the Tunnel prior to 1930, a trip to one of the nearby caves was part of the experience. The cave most often mentioned by these visitors is today referred to as Bolling Cave, even though this spelling is incorrect. As in many sciences, speleology included, whenever a name is used first, that name has right of precedence. Near Pennington Gap in Lee County, Virginia, there is a beautiful cave, mapped and described in literature before the one near the Tunnel, spelled "Bowling." Early deeds around the Natural Tunnel area refer to an early settler named "Bowlin"; later deeds added the "g." This settler gave the cave near the Tunnel its name. But "Bowling"

conflicted with the cave near Pennington Gap, so the spelling was altered to "Bolling," which is how it is listed in cave literature today. For our purposes, this cave will be called "Bowlin."

Bowlin Cave is located approximately 1,500 feet northwest of the North Portal (see Figure 57), at an elevation of 1,588 feet above sea level. The cave has a total surveyed passage of 1,863 feet, and a total vertical extent (i.e., total relief, from highest to lowest point) of 55 feet (see Figure 58).

For most of its distance, Bowlin is a "walking" cave, but some crawling is required to access the southern half, and the southernmost end of the cave requires a belly crawl through a bear wallow. Claw marks in the mud pit at this point testify to a hibernating bear making this, at some point, his winter home. There is no indication Bowlin was worked for saltpeter.

It appears that most early visitors to Bowlin Cave, after stooping through the entrance (see Figure 59), contented themselves with a short walk into the entrance room and rimstone area beyond, still within sight of the entrance. This is especially true of the Victorian era, when full skirts did not allow for more strenuous endeavors (see Figure 60).

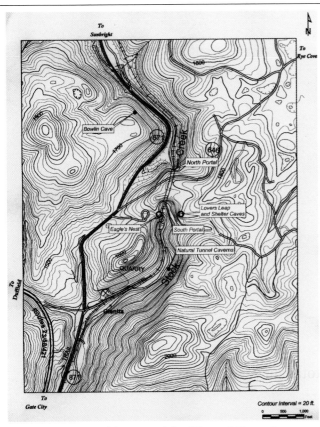

Figure 57. Topographic map of the Natural Tunnel area, with prominent features noted. (Courtesy of Geographic Information Development)

But more adventurous types did explore the cave to its full extent. As was true of much early cave exploration (which is, unfortunately, still true in many unprotected caves today), visitors would write their names on formations. Though vandalism in the cave is illegal now, these old signatures (see Figure 61) offer a tantalizing glimpse into those early days. The following is a partial list of names and dates transcribed from Bowlin Cave, listing only those which are distinct, as incrustation by mud and calcite has rendered many of the names unreadable. Many dates begin with "18," but the last two numbers are vague. Many dates in the 1950s are present, but not all are listed here. Question marks denote unreadable portions.

- 1817 (This date is clearly legible, but as such, is suspect.)
- (? unreadable name) 1857
- April 7, 1861 (possibly 1867) Ada or Ida Cole
- Bob Stone 1863 Frances Anderson (See Figure 62)
- DB 1876 (Apparently written with candle smoke, and certainly not Daniel Boone! See Figure 63)
- J R Forgy (?) 1877
- 1878 O? Schu?
- Mrs. M. M. Phipp Geo? Phipp 1883
- N R Hicks, 1883
- W A Head July (?), 1892
- 1894 J M (following is a date of 189?)
- VA-TN 1899
- H. Allison Oct. 24, 1903
- 1906 Mr. H. C. Paw?
- Mrs. J. H. Ha?, San Diego, Calif. 1907
- Lettie Brown 1908
- H. A. Favre July 23, 1910, Portsmouth, Ohio Mildred Prichard L. D. Prichard (See Figure 64)
- (? unreadable name) 1912
- March 30, 1912, Mrs. J. (?) Testa, Husker, TN
- Mary Kate (?), (?) Virginia (?) Mar. 11, 1915
- S. C. Thomas 1918
- Howard Jones, Sept. 18, 1921
- Big Stone, VA (Many examples, simply reading as this, are present.)
- J H Starnes
- 1958 Bernie Olinger, Kathleen Olinger, Catherine Olinger
- Gate City, May 26, 196? S. Whaley
- 5/3/96

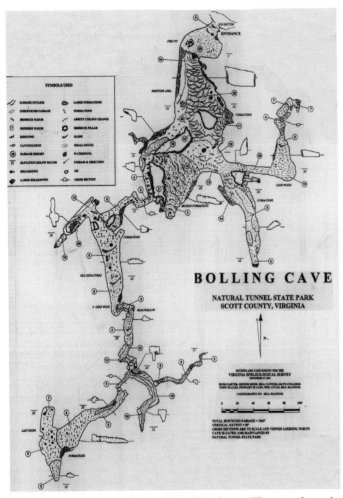

BOLLING CAVE

NATURAL TUNNEL STATE PARK
SCOTT COUNTY, VIRGINIA

Figure 58. Map of Bolling (Bowlin) Cave. The numbers in circles refer to the ceiling height at the point noted. The numbers with lines above indicate the elevation in feet that point is below datum, in this case, the entrance. The area noted as "Old Signatures" is the area of the cave where visitors have written their names on formations. Cartography by Bill Balfour. (Courtesy of the Virginia Speleological Survey)

Figure 59. Entrance to Bowlin Cave. The cave is gated and locked by Natural Tunnel State Park. The gate seen here is a bat gate, which allows free movement of bats but prevents entrance of the most destructive mammal to frequent caves, man. (Photograph by Stewart Scales)

Figure 60. Postcard, circa 1900, of "Bowling Cave." Many of the formations in this view have been destroyed by vandals. (From Natural Tunnel State Park files)

Looking out of the South Portal

The North Portal

The South Portal

The South Portal from above

This wheel pumped water from a spring for Natural Tunnel patrons.

Figure 62. Stone and Anderson visited Bowlin Cave during the Civil War, perhaps scouting for a source of saltpeter. (Photograph by Leslie Bright)

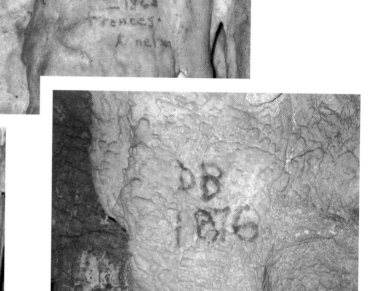

Figure 63. This signature and date were written with candle smoke. (Photograph by Leslie Bright)

Figure 61. This stalactite in Bowlin Cave is covered with signatures in pencil, as are many nearby formations. Due to mud encrustation and continued formation growth, many are becoming unreadable. (Photograph by Leslie Bright)

Figure 64. The Favre and Prichard party, from Portsmouth, Ohio, visited Bowlin Cave on July 23, 1910, and left these signatures. (Photograph by Leslie Bright)

Unfortunately, and as is true with many caves, vandalism and formation destruction have occurred in Bowlin Cave. The cave is now a part of, and gated and controlled by, Natural Tunnel State Park. Fittingly, wild cave tours are now offered by the Park Service, coming full circle to the experience of early Tunnel visitors, where exploration of the "Cave of the Unknown" was part of the tour.

The Natural Tunnel Caverns are located approximately 1,650 feet south of the South Portal, on the east bank of Stock Creek, at an elevation of 1,330 feet above sea level (see Figure 57). The Caverns have a total surveyed passage of 766 feet and a total vertical extent of 76 feet (see Figure 65). Mostly a walking cave, two crawls are necessary, one over a large mass of roof breakdown approximately 50 feet from the entrance, and another about 300 feet from the cave's terminus (a tubular, twisting, and climbing passage sometimes referred to as "Scales's Torment").

An intermittent stream that, in wet seasons, spills over the cave entrance (see Figure 66) apparently feeds a lovely waterfall present inside the cave. Water exits the cave in a swallow hole approximately 180 feet from the entrance, at or near the elevation of nearby Stock Creek. This water has to resurge into Stock Creek, but the exact point has not been ascertained.

The Caverns (sometimes referred to as Pannell Cave, after a former owner) are reported by locals to have been used as a speakeasy during Prohibition. While no excavation for saltpeter is obvious, a mud-filled area just inside the entrance (see Figure 67) has been dug out, and old wagon ruts are still evident. Like Bowlin Cave, the Caverns have been vandalized, but the entrance is now gated and controlled by Natural Tunnel State Park, which offers cave tours.

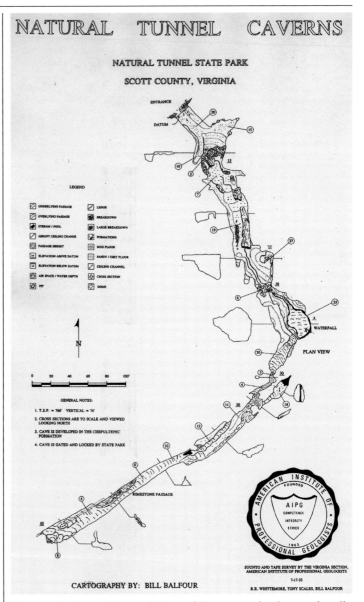

Figure 65. Map of Natural Tunnel Caverns, also known locally as Pannell Cave. The underscored numbers indicate the elevation in feet of that point above datum, in this case, the entrance. Note how most of this cave, as opposed to Bowlin Cave, is above the entrance, and that the end of the cave is 65 feet higher than the entrance. Cartography by Bill Balfour. (Courtesy of the Virginia Section of the American Institute of Professional Geologists)

The Shelter Caves (see Figure 68) are a series of four caves along the eastern Amphitheater wall at an elevation of 1,625 feet above sea level, 300 feet above the valley floor, and 100 feet below Lover's Leap. These four caves total 183 feet in length. The largest and southernmost (see Figures 69-71) is called Big Shelter Cave, the longest at nearly 100 feet. Likely due to their remote location and multiple avenues of exit (it would take a number of men on the ridge above and in the valley below to surround these caves), they were used for "ribald and bawdy" activity in times past, particularly gambling. Unlike Bowlin Cave, visitors here inscribed their names in the stone itself (see Figures 72 and 73). Because of difficult access on very steep and loose ground, these caves are not open to public visitation.

Numerous solution cavities are present in the Amphitheater walls, but most are small and inaccessible. A small cave at stream level on the west side of the South Portal (see Figure 74) is locally called "Saltpeter Cave," but no peter dirt is present in this cave, which is only about 30 feet in length. The entrance to the cave is hidden from view at track level by a large talus pile from rockfall from the Amphitheater wall, and possibly from deposition of material during railroad construction.

Figure 66. View of Natural Tunnel Caverns from the west bank of Stock Creek, March 2002. Normally, the cascading stream seen here falls as a fine spray over the entrance and is usually dry during the late summer and fall. Some portion of this stream likely enters the roof of the cave to feed a waterfall inside. (Photograph by Craig Seaver)

Figure 67. The entrance to Natural Tunnel Caverns. Like Bowlin Cave, this cave has a metal bat gate.

Figure 69. A view of Lover's Leap and the Tower from near the Eagle's Nest. The Shelter Caves are a series of four caves below Lover's Leap.

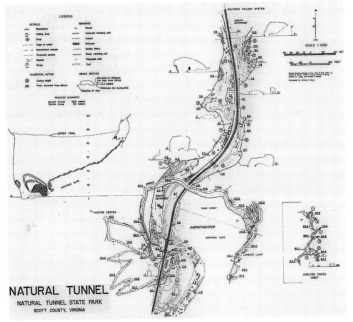

Figure 68. Map of Natural Tunnel, with an inset showing the Shelter Caves. Note that when this wonderful map was made, in 1977, Southern still served the South. Cartography by William C. Douty. (Courtesy of the Virginia Speleological Survey)

Figure 70. The entrance to Big Shelter Cave, the southern-most in the series of four caves. It is not possible to get a direct photograph into the cave because of a sheer drop-off. (Photograph by Leslie Bright)

SIDE TRAILS

Andrew Jackson Pearcy was a railroad surveyor who lived in Speers Ferry and kept a diary of personal and business-related matters. His entry for August 10, 1902, though brief, paints a picture of the Tunnel experience at that time: "Went to Tunnel & Cave. All had dinner at Mouth Cave. Had a Banjo and a nice dance in Ball Room. Little Fat was first best dancer." Little Fat was a friend of Pearcy, and it must have been an interesting sight to see a man with that sobriquet kicking up his heels in Bowlin Cave.

The name "J. M. McElroy" is beautifully inscribed in one of the Shelter Caves (see Figure 72). One J. M. McElroy was listed as a delegate to the Virginia General Assembly, representing Lee and Wise counties, in the 1863-1864 session. This session was held in the capital of the Confederacy, Richmond.

Besides a walk through the Tunnel and a trip to a cave, one other requisite part of the visit was a stroll to Lover's Leap. Affording probably the grandest

Figure 72. Unlike Bowlin Cave, visitors to the Shelter Caves, perhaps whiling away time between games of chance, inscribed their names in the rock. It is obvious here that J. M. McElroy had a lot of time and a sharp penknife, if not a chisel. (Photograph by Leslie Bright)

view of the Tunnel, at least for earthbound mortals, one could not say he had "done the Tunnel" if he had not peered into that chasm over the brink of Lover's Leap, which is still a bit unnerving today, even with cyclone fencing in place.

But, for a select few, Lover's Leap was the sole intent of the visit. Many a couple has tied the knot on this precipice, no doubt giddy with love and the romance of tragic, plummeting lovers. One such story, common in the early days, is of Miss Schaffer and Mister Lane. In 1915, Miss Schaffer was a teacher at the Manville School of Gate City. At that time, to be a teacher in Scott County, one had to be bright, clean, forthright—and single. Determined to marry Mister Lane, however, Miss Schaffer was no fool, though a bit anxious.

Waiting until just before the end of the school year—not wanting to forfeit her pay for breach of contract—Miss Schaffer sprang her plan into action. Using a "chance" (read as well planned) visit by her

Figure 71. Looking out of Big Shelter Cave. (From the files of Natural Tunnel State Park)

beau's sister and brothers on the next-to-last day before commencement, she indicated to the school management that, as she had to meet a "friend" the next day in Gate City, she would spend the night at her visitors' home, the better to get an early start to meet that friend.

That next day, Miss Schaffer met not one but two friends—Mister Lane, of course, and her preacher, privy and agreeable to the plot. And they met not at Gate City but at the railroad station, Mister Lane at the Gate City station, and the good preacher at the Albert station three miles down the line. By chance, they encountered another preacher, a friend of Miss Schaffer's preacher, at the Albert station. He inquired of the two why Miss Schaffer was leaving before commencement and asked about his brother preacher's itinerary, almost giving the game away. Miss Schaffer simply stated that she was leaving early for home, and her preacher to be with his flock, and they managed to make the V&SW train and their escape.

The purveyor of this tale, the sister to Mister Lane, ended the story this way: "At half past twelve we wound around the east Tunnel and climbed up quite a distance on it and found a beautiful level spot facing that big rock known as 'Lover's Leap.' Then and there two lovers made a fatal leap into matrimony and thus ended the romance." I am unsure if Mister Lane's sister meant to end the story with these words, but I couldn't have phrased it better.

Figure 73. Just below Mr. McElroy's inscription, Mr. Kelly recorded the year of his visit, 1859. It gives one pause to think where these gentlemen would be two years later. (Photograph by Leslie Bright)

Figure 74. The entrance to the so-called Saltpeter Cave is just above stream level and partially hidden by a talus pile at the South Portal. Nothing has indicated that this cave was ever worked for saltpeter. (Photograph by Craig Seaver)

THERE'S GOTTA BE A WAY TO MAKE A BUCK
THE NATURAL TUNNEL AND CAVERNS CORPORATION, 1928-1939

WELL NOW I CANNOT TELL IT ALL, THERE IS TOO MUCH FOR ME / SO IF YOU WANT TO KNOW THE REST JUST COME OUT HERE AND SEE. / SO RISE UP EARLY, FIX YOUR LUNCH IN A GREAT BIG BUNDLE, / GET IN YOU CAR AND DRIVE AWAY TO THIS MANIFICIENT [SIC] NATURAL TUNNEL.

—MRS. E. H. WALKER, GRAND OPENING ADDRESS, AUGUST 25, 1931

W. James (and company) had grand designs, but to no avail. The SA&O planned to develop the property, even bring in electricity, but the Tunnel was lost to them in the shuffle of the big business cards. The V&SW treated the Tunnel as an occasional draw for its excursion trains, a piddling money-maker at best. To make a buck off this place would take some thinking, some planning, and some investment. It would take Elbert H. Walker.

If he was anything, E. H. Walker was a businessman. Born in Greene County, Tennessee, in 1860, Walker started life as a carpenter, saving his funds toward opening a business. How he, his wife, Julia A., and his children (there were five, eventually) came to Glenita is uncertain, but by 1900, Walker was firmly ensconced in trade in that community.

In Glenita, Walker owned the only general store, owned up to three sawmills in the area, and had considerable landholdings in the Stock Creek Valley. Near his home and store, he financed the building of the Glenita Free Will Baptist Church, which still stands today. Immediately adjacent to the church, he leased property for a quarry that operated for nearly 70 years (which was donated to Natural Tunnel State Park by the Walker heirs in 1987).

Walker entered into a contract with V&SW in March of 1905, whereby he agreed to build a combination store and depot building on railroad property. The contract stipulated that Walker would erect the structure at his own expense but would have the exclusive use of the building for 10 years, as long as he cooperated with the railroad in passenger and freight care and guaranteed he would not "traffic, or permit others to traffic, in intoxicants upon the premises."

It is unknown if this combination depot/store was built; by the mid-1910s, Walker was operating out of his own building (see Figure 75), and the Glenita Depot was located across the tracks from the store (see Figure 76) and the nearby water tank (see Figure 77). But no matter—if Walker couldn't have the depot, he'd have the Tunnel!

Figure 75. The community of Glenita, circa 1918. E. H. Walker's home is to the left of view; six years later it would burn to the ground (the cut-stone foundation, with a new home on top, is still visible today). The Glenita Free Will Baptist Church is just left of the water tank in the distance. Right of the water tank and adjacent to the tracks (Southern Railway by this time) is E. H. Walker's store. The Glenita Depot is just out of view to the right. It is always interesting to note the extent of cleared land in Southwest Virginia in photographs of this period. (Photograph donated to Natural Tunnel State Park by Ron Walker, grandson of E. H. Walker)

It is plausible that Walker, running the only general store in the immediate area, was the supplier of victuals for the early excursion trains visiting the Tunnel. Certainly, a wayward traveler wanting to visit the Tunnel would stop by the store for supplies and directions. As such, being the consummate businessman, Walker would recognize that money could be made if he could control the whole kit and caboodle.

By deed dated December 15, 1908, Walker purchased "three hundred and thirty-eight and twenty-seven one-hundredths (338.27) acres, more or less" from the Interstate Coal & Iron Company, which included W. W. James and company's original Natural Tunnel tract. The cost was $1,000 cash in hand paid, with a balance of $2,000 to be paid by June 1,

1909. Walker paid off the balance by November. He owned the Tunnel.

What Walker did with the property—that is, how he earned money from it during 1908-1925—is unknown. It does not appear that any improvements to the infrastructure were made. Walker's purchase would have included the Pavilion; it's plausible he was taking a cut from excursion-train fares, and you can bet his store would have been the source of refreshments after he owned the Pavilion outright. Otherwise, it appears unlikely admission was charged, as there was no way to control access to the property.

Perhaps the Tunnel simply served as an enticement, and Walker hoped Tunnel visitors would also visit his store. There is record that his son, Kyle, served as a guide for the nearby Bowlin Cave during this time. Perhaps guiding visitors to, and through, the Tunnel provided some income. However, in 1924, the Walker home burned to the ground, a vic-

Figure 76. Glenita Depot, circa 1930. The view is to the southwest, down the tracks to Clinchport. The Southern Railway water tank is in the distance. (Courtesy of Kenny Fannon)

Figure 77. Southern Engine 4053 takes on water at the Glenita water tank in preparation to run the Tunnel, circa 1930. (Courtesy of Kenny Fannon)

tim of sparks from the wood stove on a split-shake roof. Walker bought a small farm near Gate City, built a new home, sold his business, moved his family, and retired.

But once a businessman, always a businessman. Now in the county seat, Walker was in greater contact with the leaders of Scott County. He was approached by three prominent businessmen, Edmonds D. Rollins (a general practitioner), W. H. Perry (a dentist, later a state delegate), and Belt H. Quillen (livestock, lumber, and real estate), who urged Walker to consider developing the Tunnel property as a tour-

ist attraction. Walker promptly sold ¾ interest in the property (70 acres including the Tunnel) to these gentlemen by deed dated September 10, 1925. Each man gave an equal share toward the $9,000 selling price, payable by September 30, 1930.

Operation of the tourist attraction stumbled, at first. A small building on the west side of Stock Creek, south of the Little Tunnel near Pannell Cave (now Natural Tunnel Caverns), served as headquarters. Visitors, who reached the site by train to the Glenita Depot or by driving, were charged 50 cents each—not a small price for the time—but the service included a guide, usually a youngster from one of the owners' families. Nabs and pop were five cents a throw; lavatory facilities were the nearest tree. Open only on weekends, the operation, needless to say, was not a cash cow.

Determined to make their enterprise profitable, on October 13, 1928, the owners incorporated under the name of Natural Tunnel and Caverns Corporation (NT&CC), deeding their ¼ ownerships to the corporation, with E. D. Rollins as president and W. H. Perry as secretary. Not wasting any time, that same day, the NT&CC entered into a lease agreement with Joseph P. Seaton of Johnson City, Tennessee. The agreement stated that Seaton would "expend the sum of at least Ten Thousand ($10,000.00) dollars on the development of said property during the year 1929." Seaton set up a new corporation, The Natural Tunnel Amusement Company (NTAC) and set about his business.

Seaton's business promptly failed. To students of history, the salient phrase in the agreement above is "during the year 1929." The NT&CC owners, one retired and the others engaged in their businesses, rightly recognized they needed a second party to improve and manage the Natural Tunnel operation. The timing, admittedly in hindsight, could not have been worse. On October 29, 1929—Black Tuesday—the U.S. stock market crashed. While it would be presumptuous to say the crash was the only cause of the failure of Seaton's company, by the end of 1929, little cash was available, and certainly the casual tourist was retrenching for a long, cold winter.

The lease with Seaton was terminated on January 28, 1930, for his failure to expend the agreed-upon sum. The termination, however, did include a payment of $1,800 to Seaton for two acres of land he had purchased for the NTAC. This land is Seaton's one tangible contribution to the history of Natural Tunnel—he purchased the tract that would serve the NT&CC as the visitors entrance (which now serves as the entranceway to Natural Tunnel State Park), thus setting the stage for visitor access to the Tunnel from above, as opposed to the years of access from the Stock Creek Valley and the confines of the railroad bed.

The NT&CC is known to have issued stock (see Figure 78), but whether or not the stock generated sufficient capital, or the owners dipped into their own pockets, changes were made. While visitors still accessed the Tunnel from the little shack by Stock Creek and ate their nickel Nabs, improvements were going on above, culminating in a flurry of activity in 1931. Kyle Walker put it this way: "Cecil Quillen, Jamie Seaver and I spent the entire summer of 1931 working at Natural Tunnel. We 'batched' and it took a cast iron stomach to digest some of the meals we turned out on a two-burner camp stove. The original building, many of the trails and some of the fences were the results of our sweat and toil and I will always feel that a part of me still lingers in those old hills around the tunnel."

The activity resulted in an entrance road, a small caretakers house, a gift shop (see Figure 79), toilet facilities, a trail to Lover's Leap (referred to in the old deeds as Table Rock), a switchback trail to Stock Creek and the railroad tracks (visitors would access the Natural Tunnel via the Little Tunnel, crossing the plate girder over Stock Creek), and an impressive amount of fencing (see Figure 80). The latter was particularly needed. With the center of activity now above the Tunnel, it wouldn't do to have a paying visitor fall to the bottom!

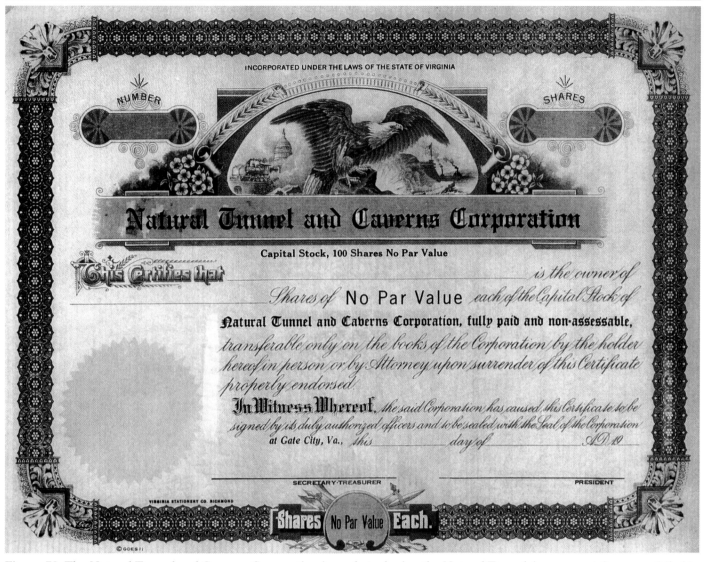

INCORPORATED UNDER THE LAWS OF THE STATE OF VIRGINIA

NUMBER

SHARES

Natural Tunnel and Caverns Corporation

Capital Stock, 100 Shares No Par Value

This Certifies that _____ is the owner of

_____ Shares of **No Par Value** each of the Capital Stock of

Natural Tunnel and Caverns Corporation, fully paid and non-assessable, transferable only on the books of the Corporation by the holder hereof in person or by Attorney upon surrender of this Certificate properly endorsed.

In Witness Whereof, the said Corporation has caused this Certificate to be signed by its duly authorized officers and to be sealed with the Seal of the Corporation at Gate City, Va., this _____ day of _____ A.D. 19

SECRETARY-TREASURER   PRESIDENT

VIRGINIA STATIONERY CO. RICHMOND

Shares No Par Value Each.

© GOES 11

Figure 78. The Natural Tunnel and Caverns Corporation issued stock after the Natural Tunnel Amusement Company failed in 1930, in an effort to generate working capital. (From the files of Natural Tunnel State Park)

On August 25, 1931, the NT&CC held their grand opening. Admission was $1 a head. The festivities were broadcast over the only radio station in the area, WOPI of Bristol, Tennessee, which later would be famous for the start of the career of Tennessee Ernie Ford. Kyle Walker and friends provided string-band music, and his mother, Julia A. Walker, read a poem written expressly for the occasion (see Figure 81).

During the NT&CC proprietorship, the facility was primarily run by Lyle and Dalla Alley. Dalla ran the gift shop, and Lyle, who was also the Scott County

Figure 79. For years, Natural Tunnel was accessed via the Stock Creek Valley and the railroad tracks. Joseph Seaton acquired access off Route 646 in 1930 for the Natural Tunnel Amusement Company. In 1931, trails and rudimentary picnic areas were built, and the center of activity shifted to above the Tunnel and around the new gift shop, seen here. This picture, circa the early 1930s, must be before Labor Day, as everyone is wearing white. (From the files of Natural Tunnel State Park)

Figure 80. This postcard shows the gift shop and parking area, with a view to Lover's Leap, mid-1930s. The Natural Tunnel and Caverns Corporation built an impressive amount of fencing to save wandering tourists from a plunge into the Amphitheater, a luxury not afforded one unfortunate circuit preacher (discussed in Chapter 14).

POEM WRITTEN AND BROADCAST OVER RADIO STATION W O P I, BRISTOL, VIRGINIA, BY MRS. E. H. (JULIA A.) WALKER ON SUNDAY, AUGUST 25, 1931
From Natural Tunnel

Hello folks from everywhere, to one and all I'll say
Out here at Natural Tunnel we are having one great day
We are having such a lovely time I'll bet right now that you
Are wishing you were here with us - well that is my wish too.

But thanks to WOPI they have made a way
though you're not with us you can hear what each one has to say.
Of all the places in the State, or any state I'll say
Natural Tunnel is the best to have an outing day.

We have a place to park your cars; a lovely picnic ground
And tables made to spread your lunch where it's shady all around.
Then there is water right at hand - a most important thing
There is no better for it flows from a pure and crystal spring.

Now you can rest assured, we are doing all we can do
To give you a hearty welcome here and make things nice for you.
And Oh! such beautiful scenery - the best in all the land,
And just to know it all was made by God's almighty hand

Stock Creek runs through this tunnel, the railroad runs through too;
The state road runs right over the top. I think that's grand don't you?
The entire length of the tunnel is some 900 feet,
The average width of passage way is one hundred, thirty feet.

The outside walls are rugged and so high, up to four hundred feet
And still higher where Winoah stood to make her fatal leap.
One day along came Isaac Wolfe and stood gazing up so high.
He said I believe I could climb on top; If you will help me I will try.

They placed a pulley up so high and from this a rope was dropped
Then tied old Ike on the other end and pulled him to the top.
Then came along two bridge builders who looked much like a clown;
They said, now you have pulled a man up we will show you how to come down.

They stretched two ropes from the top and after looking all around
They clasped these ropes in their hands and started coming down.
And while descending on these ropes a hundred feet they came
And then they stopped and on that stone each one wrote his name.

And don't you know that after this they turned right around
And down and down and down they came until they reached the ground.
There are caverns very near, so new and yet so old,
They are a thing of beauty, most wondrous to behold.

They have stalagmites growing up and stalactites growing down
Many things beyond description showered with beauty all around.
Then there is another feature, a nice dance hall
Where people used to gather to have an old time ball.

Well now I cannot tell it all, there is too much for me
So if you want to know the rest just come out here and see.
So rise up early, fix your lunch into a great big bundle,
Get in your car and drive away to this manificent Natural Tunnel.

              Mrs. E. H. (Julia A.) Walker

Figure 81. The grand opening of Natural Tunnel, under the auspices of the Natural Tunnel and Caverns Corporation, was held on August 25, 1931. WOPI of Bristol, Virginia—the only radio station in the area—broadcast the event. Besides music, the festivities included this wonderfully quaint poem by Julia A. Walker, wife of part owner Elbert H. Walker. Courtesy of Ruby Stewart, granddaughter of Julia and Elbert Walker. It is my opinion, from the warm recollections provided by Mrs. Stewart, that Julia Walker was the epitome of the Southern grandmother.

game warden, served as a "special policeman" for the NT&CC. Use of the Shelter Caves near Lover's Leap as a gambling den was popular, and of course, 'shine still flowed in the hills. According to Jack Quillen, it was a popular pastime for the local roughnecks to get liquored up and start fights with Mr. Alley.

With controllable access, infrastructure, and amenities, Natural Tunnel, via the NT&CC, was finally a viable operation (though not a big money-maker, as it was open only during the summer months). But visitors came, paid their admission, ate their Nabs, bought their trinkets, and sent postcards home (see Figures 82 and 83). And so it went for seven years.

Then comes one of the ironies of the Natural Tunnel story. Since day one, when the first words were printed about the Tunnel, no author could help but compare the gargantuan country cousin to the smaller but more famous Natural Bridge. By 1937 or 1938, the glow of their new enterprise had dimmed somewhat to the owners of the NT&CC. They packed their bags and headed northeast on a road trip, stopping off at the Virginia Military Institute to pick up Belt Quillen's son, Jack, who became the driver for the remainder of the trip.

The group then drove to Natural Bridge and there offered the property and facilities of the NT&CC—Natural Tunnel—for sale to the Natural Bridge Corporation! The Natural Bridge Corporation declined, stating that the Tunnel was simply too remote, both from their operation and the general public, to be practicable.

Undaunted, the travelers took a more easterly course, stopped at Williamsburg, and there made the same offer to the new Williamsburg Foundation! Though certainly capable of making the purchase,

NATURAL TUNNEL, 14 MILES W. OF GATE CITY, VA., ON U. S. 23 2N-12

Figure 82. This postcard, dated 1937, shows the South Portal during the Natural Tunnel and Caverns Corporation period. The Pavilion had been gone for probably over 15 years. (Courtesy of Jack Quillen)

Figure 83. This wonderful series of linen postcards (including the one on the next page) from the 1930s appears to portray Natural Tunnel as a Hawaiian paradise as opposed to a temperate-latitude jewel.

508:—NATURAL TUNNEL, IN SOUTHWESTERN VIRGINIA.

Figure 83 (cont.)

backed by Rockefeller money, the foundation declined, citing the same reasons as the Natural Bridge Corporation plus the observation that, while the Tunnel might fit with the Natural Bridge operation, it would be difficult to mesh with the foundation's goals. Natural Tunnel remained in the hands of Southwest Virginians.

SIDE TRAILS

Fencing from the Eagle's Nest to Lover's Leap not only provided security for visitors on those heights, but also for those below. It seems to be human nature to want to throw an object from a height, and while the fencing did not stop this prac-

tice at Natural Tunnel (it is still a problem today), it did quell the activity somewhat. Andrew Jackson Pearcy, in his diary entry for September 21, 1902, tells us of a pre-fence occurrence: "Went to Tunnel to picnic from Mountain City Tenn. Ebb Walker [E. H. Walker] was hit with rock some one throwed from top of tunnel. Hit in eye."

As a final note on E. H. Walker's earliest relationship to the Tunnel, the "Personals" column in the May 16, 1907, issue of the *Gate City Herald* notes, "Squire E. H. Walker was up from Natural Tunnel. He formerly conducted a successful mercantile business at that place." This statement implies that Walker may have had a store for a short while immediately at the Tunnel, as opposed to the later and longer-lived store at Glenita.

Apparently a favorite subject, Mr. Walker was frequently mentioned in the *Gate City Herald*. For example, the January 7, 1932, issue ran an article entitled "Watermelon Found on New Year's Eve," stating, "Still as green, in color, as it was back in the early fall, a watermelon was found in the garden near the home of E. H. Walker, four miles west of here shortly before new years eve. Walker explained that the melon was being kept for doubters' benefit, and that it was located under a fodder shock in the midst of a large layer of green grass."

WHERE HAS ALL THE WATER GONE?
OBSERVATIONS OF STOCK CREEK THROUGH THE TUNNEL

I HAVE BEEN TOLD THAT THE WATER AT HIGH TIDE RUSHES THROUGH THE TUNNEL WITH TERRIFIC SWIFTNESS, AND I COULD ALMOST SEE, "IN MY MIND'S EYE," THE HISSING, WHIRLING WAVES, AND HEAR THEM AS THEY LASHED THE GRANITE WALLS IN MAD FURY. IMMENSE LOGS AND DRIFT-WOOD WERE LEFT HIGH AND DRY, AND GAVE TOKEN OF THE FEARFUL TIMES THAT HAD BEEN.

—UNNAMED CORRESPONDENT TO THE *RICHMOND DAILY WHIG*, SEPTEMBER 14, 1872

arly visitors to Natural Tunnel were usually in such awe of its size, or afraid of falling off the Amphitheater walls, that any reference to Stock Creek was in passing, though some almost made the leap of logic and attributed this poor little creek with something to do with the Tunnel's formation. When they did write of the creek, they couldn't help but speak of it in poetic terms.

Colonel Long, of his 1831 visit, wrote, "The extent of the tunnel from its upper to its lower extremity, following its meanders, is about 150 yards, in which distance the stream falls about ten feet, emitting, in its passage over a rocky bed, an agreeable murmur, which is rendered more grateful by its reverberations upon the roof and sides of the grotto."

In 1870, after nearly stumbling over himself describing the grand scene, R. L. Bachman wrote, "But our little creek must not be forgotton [sic]. Still babbling still tumbling, it approaches the dark frowning bluff on the north. Like the visitor, it finds a provision made by nature. Like him, it timidly enters the wide, gloomy channel and feels its way along the walls and around the curves till fairly through the tunnel. Then, as if gladdened by the daylight, 'it slips between the ridges,' and hastens by the woody hills 'to join the brimming river.'"

However, in 1871, Edward Pollard described his visit to the Tunnel, with no Stock Creek in it! He noted, "The bed of the stream, from which the water has disappeared on account of the drouth [sic], the reduced currents sinking to lower subterranean channels, is piled with great irregular rocks, on the sharp points of which we stumble and cut our hands...."

Of course, streams do dry up because of drought, but Emile Low, telling of his 1893 visit to the Tunnel, only added to the enigma. He observed, "at the present time there exists an underground passage, which begins about one-eighth of a mile above the Natural

Tunnel, and ends about one-quarter of a mile below it. When the stream gets low, nearly all the water passes through this underground outlet and its issue is plainly discernible below the tunnel at several different points. One outlet is in the bed of the stream, where it bubbles up like a miniature geyser. . . ."

Stock Creek is a bedrock stream (see Figure 84), that is, it flows on bedrock and not on alluvial fill, though fill is present along the stream banks. Before railroad construction, when the Tunnel was still choked with rocks and debris, it is entirely possible that Stock Creek, at low flow, could pass under and through this material unobserved. In 1855, a student magazine at Emory and Henry College published an account of a visit to the Tunnel that states, "we went beneath the roof. The stream, in truth, hid itself for it sank out of sight and was still. . . ," implying, though couched in poetic terms, that the stream had disappeared into the rock fill.

Mr. Low, however, who provides us with keen observations of the Tunnel and its surroundings just after railroad construction, has left us with a real puzzle. No indication of an "underground outlet" upstream of the North Portal has ever been observed, nor below the South Portal a "miniature geyser," though certainly there are springs and seeps along the Stock Creek Valley. Interestingly, during the writing of this book in the late summer and early fall of 2002, Stock Creek went dry just downstream of Natural Tunnel Caverns but not through the Tunnel, for a distance of about 200 feet (see Figure 85), and did not flow again before a spring that enters from the north bank of the creek supplied sufficient water. This is roughly the same area of resurgence of flow indicated by Low.

Dissolution of the bedrock has occurred, and

Figure 84. Stock Creek, seen here east of the plate girder in midsummer, flows on bedrock in the vicinity of Natural Tunnel. Just downstream of here is the presumed location of Emile Low's "geyser." (Photograph by Leslie Bright)

continues to occur, at and below Stock Creek. Solution tubes may be present along fractures under the creek and, of course, under the Tunnel. If the water level in the creek is diminished by drought, an upstream swallet (swallow hole) could capture all of the flow and divert it into these tubes, where it could rise back to the streambed farther downstream.

The railroad removed most, if not all, of the debris in the Tunnel and its portals and likely used material dredged from Stock Creek all along its route for bedding material. In the immediate area of the Tunnel, by construction of the railroad grade and retaining walls, Stock Creek was forced into a new channel. It is possible that Mr. Low observed the results of that work, and for a short time, Stock Creek flowed through new or recently uncovered fractures, but if so, they have long since filled and healed. Regretfully, no miniature Old Faithful is there today to add to the mystique of Natural Tunnel.

Figure 85. Looking up Stock Creek, just below the bridge crossing to Natural Tunnel Caverns, in August of 2002. Compare this view to Figure 84.

Figure 86. Water from a "pure and crystal spring," just left of view, was run by flume to this wheel, which powered a ram pump and supplied water to the old Natural Tunnel Lodge, later the original visitors center. The supply became unpotable due to drainage from the picnic area. The North Portal is just over the ridge in the background.

SIDE DRAIN

The movement of water underground in karst terrain can be mysterious, even with detailed scientific study. Sometimes the question is not so much "Where has the water gone?" but "Where has the water been?" This question was, unfortunately, answered when the Park was forced to abandon its water supply in the 1980s. The spring used then (likely the "pure and crystal spring" of Julia Walker's poem) is located northeast of the North Portal (see Figure 86), and for years, via a ram pump, supplied water to the old visitors center and lodge (later the new visitors center).

However, when the picnic and parking areas were constructed, dye tracing showed that water from these areas moved to the spring, rendering it impotable. A well drilled near the campground proved potable but of low yield; one drilled a few hundred feet away solved the problem, proving both potable and of enormous yield, confirming the axiom that, in karst terrain, "Water is where you find it."

Surprisingly, you can find water at the very edge of the cliff above Natural Tunnel Caverns, some 300 feet above Stock Creek. The small stream that falls over the caverns (see Chapter 9 and Figure 66) originates at a series of springs. These springs probably served as the water source for an old homestead nearby, now grown over, with only the hand-laid rocks of the foundation and part of the chimney left. A small graveyard there has at least eight, and possibly as many as ten, graves, now sunken depressions. Attesting to the age of these graves are the headstones, which are nothing more than local native rock, rough and weather-beaten, with no inscriptions, just simple markers noting that someone rests there.

THERE'S GOTTA BE A WAY TO MAKE MORE BUCKS

THE NATURAL TUNNEL, CHASM AND CAVERNS CORPORATION, 1939-1967

ALL NATURAL TUNNEL AND ITS CAVERNS NEEDS TO MAKE IT ONE OF THE BEST KNOWN SPOTS IN THIS MOUNTAIN SECTION, IS MONEY AND MANAGEMENT.

—BRISTOL CHAMBER OF COMMERCE LETTER IN SUPPORT OF THE NATURAL TUNNEL, CHASM AND CAVERNS CORPORATION, DECEMBER 12, 1939

IT'S SENSATIONAL! IT'S UNBELIEVABLE! THAT THIS 87-YEAR-OLD "HUMAN FLY" ISAAC "IKE" WOLFE CAN STILL SCALE 402-FOOT WALL OF NATURAL TUNNEL JUST AS HE DID 52 YEARS AGO!

—*KINGSPORT TIMES* ADVERTISEMENT, JUNE 1941

THE COMPANY OFFERS TO THE PUBLIC FOR A REASONABLE FEE THE OPPORTUNITY TO VIEW THE EXTRAORDINARY MARVEL IN STONE OF THE ENORMOUS NATURAL TUNNEL AND THE IMMENSE AMPHITHEATRE THROUGH WHICH IT EMERGES. IN ADDITION THE TOURIST MAY BE PRIVILEGED WITH AN EXPERIENCE OF HAUNTING BEAUTY IN THE ADJACENT CAVERNS. THE COMPANY PLANS TO IMPROVE THE PROPERTY WITH A MORE ADEQUATE LODGE, COTTAGES AND/OR CABINS FOR OVERNIGHT GUESTS FOR WHICH THERE IS AN EXISTING DEMAND, RESTAURANT FACILITIES PATTERNED AFTER BRIGHT ANGEL LODGE AT GRAND CANYON, FLOOD LIGHTING, PUBLIC ADDRESS AMPLIFICATION, PROVISION OF BETTER ACCESS TO A RECENTLY DISCOVERED CAVERN, GENERAL BEAUTIFICATION, ELIMINATION OF HAZARD, ET CETERA.

—FROM THE PROSPECTUS FOR THE NATURAL TUNNEL, CHASM AND CAVERNS CORPORATION, DECEMBER 15, 1939

It has been said that the key to success, whether in love, business, or any endeavor, is timing. The NT&CC had missed the timing in their start-up, just at the beginning of the Great Depression. But they still made a go of it, found the funds, improved the property, and made a little money. Fortune would be such that their successor would try again, but again timing was miserable. It has also been said that if you can't be good, be lucky. The second time around they would be lucky.

Two eras passed in the story of Natural Tunnel in the year 1939. The Lonesome Pine Special passed through the Tunnel on its last regular trip, putting to rest the long-running promotion of the Tunnel by the railroad. From then on, the Tunnel, at least for the Southern Railway, became simply a way through the mountain. And in that year, on New Year's Day, E. H. Walker died, ending his 38-year ownership (outright and in partnership) of the Tunnel. Reorganization was necessary.

On December 8, 1939, the Natural Tunnel, Chasm and Caverns Corporation (NTC&CC) incorporated. Belt H. Quillen was president, Edmonds D. Rollins was chairman of the board (and the real taskmaster for the company), Rex R. Thompson was vice-president, Cecil D. Quillen secretary, and Samuel F. Freels treasurer. Seven days later, the company issued a prospectus (with an accompanying letter of recommendation from the Bristol Chamber of Commerce, see Figure 87) that told the story of the property to date and the plans of the directors for the future.

In 1935, the Tunnel had 4,112 visitors; by 1939, that number had doubled. Cash receipts for 1938 totaled $4,212.27, which works out to about 50 cents spent (admission and other expenditures) by each visitor. The company figured it had $1,542.83 in assets, including $202.73 cash on hand, and fixed the property's worth, counting the improvements made during the NT&CC days, at $303,693.10. Liabilities included 35,000 outstanding shares of common stock (out of 350,000 authorized), which amounted to less than 10 cents per share.

The NT&CC had tried, but the NTC&CC could do better. The company, by issuing stock ($20 a share for preferred, but only a dime a pop for common), wanted to raise funds to improve the property, particularly by the construction of "a more adequate lodge, cottages and/or cabins" and "restaurant facil-

Bristol Chamber of Commerce
INCORPORATED
BRISTOL, VA.-TENN.

December 12, 1939

Natural Tunnel, Chasm & Caverns Corp.
Gate City, Virginia

Gentlemen:

I am pleased you now plan to develop your property which for many years has attracted people from all parts of the country, even in the days when the hardships of mountain travel were experienced to reach it.

An early description of your enormous Natural Tunnel and Chasm will be found in the August 1857 number of Harpers Magazine. For over twenty years the writer has been familiar with this beauty spot and has always felt that it would be exceedingly profitable with proper financing and experienced management.

During recent years, more and more interest has been taken in this section of the United States. The tourist travel is increasing every year. The development of numerous natural wonders and beautiful mountain sections in Virginia and Tennessee, and the advertising that will be done in connection with these developments, all emphasize the fact that Natural Tunnel should be placed in a position to cash in on this movement.

As a natural wonder in Southwest Virginia, it stands alone. In the immediate vicinity, there are no influences which detract from it. The building of a State Park in upper East Tennessee is planned to be the finest in the South. This park will be located between Bristol and Kingsport and on the direct route between Bristol and the tunnel. There is also being built in the vicinity of Norton, Virginia on Route 23, a very interesting recreational area known as High Knob. This will be a national development. Natural Tunnel located as it is on U. S. Highway 23, will be between these two interesting projects.

Eastern Kentucky is interested in several developments, and the main highway from Kentucky through Cumberland Gap (a famous historic spot) is highway 58 which passes the Natural Tunnel to Gate City and Bristol. We call these matters to your attention, as they will act as additional features which draw into this territory the travelers who want to see the beauties of the Southern Appalachian Highland.

We regard the Natural Tunnel as the greatest of all of Virginia's natural wonders. It is excellently located and when fully developed, should be equally as profitable as the natural wonders farther East, many of which, as is well known, are making fortunes for their owners. All Natural Tunnel and its caverns needs to make it one of the best known spots in this mountain section, is money and management.

With best wishes for your success, I am,

Yours very truly,

W. A. Hiddleson,
Secretary

Figure 87. This letter of support, from W. A. Hiddleson, secretary of the Bristol Chamber of Commerce, accompanied the 1939 prospectus of the NTC&CC. Mr. Hiddleson's comment that all one needs is "money and management" could have been written for any project at any time in history.

ities patterned after Bright Angel Lodge at Grand Canyon, flood lighting, public address amplification, provision of better access to a recently discovered cavern. . . ." It is obvious that, after years of low-key operation, the directors wanted to "do it up right." Probably the one thing they recognized as needed was lodging. Prior to 1939, a visit to the Tunnel usually lasted only a day, though rudimentary camping was possible. And if lodging were available, visitors would want to eat more than a pop and a pack of Nabs.

The result was the Natural Tunnel Lodge, which included the restaurant and gift shop (see Figure 88). This brick structure, built below the old gift shop, had seven to eight guest rooms located in the west wing, each "fitted with the latest style and designs in furnishings. Each room [had] Beautyrest mattresses, individual tile bath and circulating hot water heat for the comfort of the occupant." In the

Figure 88. The Natural Tunnel Lodge opened its doors to the traveling public just before World War II. To the right (east) was the gift shop, the middle held the entrance and restaurant, and the left the guest rooms. Additionally, a large meeting room and walk-in freezer were downstairs.

center was the restaurant, "equipped with all-electric kitchen and dining room appliances where good food is served at reasonable prices." The gift shop was in the east wing and also served as the gateway to the hiking trails.

But, oh, the timing! Begun after the stock offering (the amount of stock sold is uncertain), something quite large and disruptive loomed in American history—World War II. With America moving toward a war footing, and the country gearing up for war-material production, there was little likelihood of a brisk tourist trade to recoup the cost of the lodge. For the next five years, until Americans had extra time, interest, and pocket money, the NTC&CC puttered along on luck.

Just before the war, in the summer of 1941, the

NTC&CC staged probably its most interesting promotional stunt. On June 15, for 83 cents for adults and 44 cents for children, tax included, visitors watched Isaac "Uncle Ike" Wolfe "scale the 402-foot wall of Natural Tunnel just as he did 52 years ago" (see Figures 89-91), while the Shoemaker High School Band of Gate City played.

Advertisement headlines of the stunt are somewhat misleading, as they used the word "scale," whereas the fine print urges visitors to view his "descent." Apparently, Uncle Ike did not climb the walls or his rope but rather was lowered by a pulley system. Rigged with a microphone, Uncle Ike broadcast his progress over WKPT radio of nearby Kingsport, Tennessee.

Before his descent, Uncle Ike told the crowd that

87-Year-Old Negotiates Natural Tunnel Wall

A tiny dot on the imposing wall of Natural Tunnel, Va., at left above, is Uncle Ike Wolf, who made his third trip down the jagged perpendicular Sunday afternoon. He dangles at the end of a rope near the arrow point. At right, willing hands grab him as he gets ready to touch his feet to the ground after the 402-foot descent. He was trussed in a harness for the trip and took time out on the way down to wave frequently at the crowds.

Photo by Thomas McNees

Figure 91. He made it!

Figure 89. Who couldn't love this face? This advertisement in the *Kingsport Times* tells of Uncle Ike's planned scaling of Natural Tunnel, but if you read the fine print, Uncle Ike will be lowered down, not climb up. Uncle Ike got a cut of the gate for his stunt.

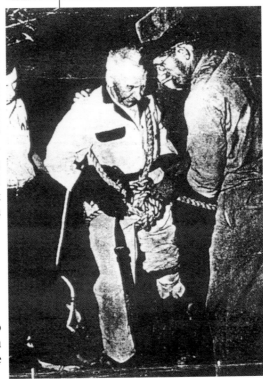

Figure 90. Suited up and ready to go, Uncle Ike prepares to go down the Amphitheater wall above the South Portal.

he had performed the same stunt 52 years earlier (1889) to investigate an eagle's nest. Whether this is true or not, "eagle's nest" reminds us of Emile Low's use of that term, and Uncle Ike's first descent coincides with SA&O construction in and through the Tunnel, and they certainly used scalers to clean the walls of the Amphitheater. Recall also that Julia A. Walker speaks of Uncle Ike in her poem. Regardless, seeing 87-year-old Uncle Ike dangling from his rope—hopefully in greater control than Poor Dotson/Dodson/Horton—would have been well worth the price of admission.

In its prospectus, the company indicates their intent to provide "better access to a recently discovered cavern." That document also lists C. Kendrick Smith, former treasurer and general manager of Endless Caverns (near New Market, Virginia, still in business today), as general manager of the Natural Tunnel property. Obviously, from the wording of the prospectus and the fact the company had hired Mr. Smith, an experienced cavern/tourist-attraction manager, the company had designs to include a caving experience—which "recently discovered cavern" is unknown—as part of the property's attractions.

Only some 15 years after the notorious Kentucky Cave Wars, the owners would be well aware of the draw of a cavern. Caving, as a part of the Natural Tunnel experience, apparently did not pan out, as Mr. Smith was with the company only a short while, replaced in 1940 by local lad Jamie Seaver, and there is no record of organized caving during the NTC&CC days, though there are certainly many signatures in Bowlin Cave dating from the 1940s and 1950s.

The prospectus also lists the intent of the company to install lighting equipment to both light the "amphitheatre" and serve a planned "spectorama." The company also planned to construct a waterfall and cascades, reported by the *Gate City Herald* to be "more than twice as high as Niagara Falls combined with color effects creating an Aurora Borealis seen only in the polar regions," as well as six cottages and ten cabins, among other improvements. These improvements did not pan out, either.

One wish that did pan out was the installation of a public-address sound system, with the main controls in the gift shop and speakers on the Amphitheater walls. If not on, as soon as a visitor paid admission and went to the trails, it was powered up. As the tourist brochure describes, "Whether the spell-bound visitor winds his way along the trails to the dizzy heights of Lover's Leap, or descends into the yawning Chasm below, delightful music, appropriate to such a setting, steals from within the deep and floats away on the breeze that follows Stock Creek towards the sea."

Visitors and former employees report the most popular recordings were "Indian Love Song" by Nelson Eddy and Jeanette McDonald, a reading of Joyce Kilmer's poem "Trees," and a reading of the legend of Lover's Leap. (How the perception of experiencing natural wonders has changed over the years—if this situation occurred today, most visitors would demand their money back!)

The Natural Tunnel, Chasm and Caverns Corporation was seeking the traveling-tourist trade. The Tunnel always seemed a victim of its remote location, so the company's brochures and prospectus were quick to point out that "Highways have at last broken their trail of progress to its very door. Today this mammoth attraction lies on the recently completed 'Great Lakes to Florida Route,' the shortest distance from

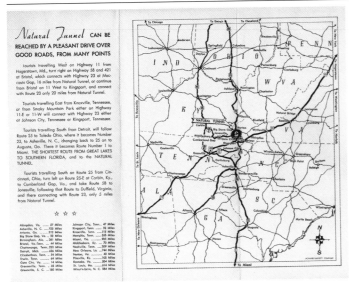

Natural Tunnel CAN BE REACHED BY A PLEASANT DRIVE OVER GOOD ROADS, FROM MANY POINTS

Tourists travelling West on Highway 11 from Hagerstown, Md., turn right on Highway 58 and 421 at Bristol, which connects with Highway 23 at Moccasin Gap, 16 miles from Natural Tunnel, or continue from Bristol on 11 West to Kingsport, and connect with Route 23 only 20 miles from Natural Tunnel.

Tourists travelling East from Knoxville, Tennessee, or from Smoky Mountain Park either on Highway 11-E or 11-W will connect with Highway 23 either at Johnson City, Tennessee or Kingsport, Tennessee.

Tourists travelling South from Detroit, will follow Route 25 to Toledo Ohio, where it becomes Number 23, to Asheville, N. C., changing back to 25 on to Augusta, Ga. There it becomes Route Number 1 to Miami. THE SHORTEST ROUTE FROM GREAT LAKES TO SOUTHERN FLORIDA, and to the NATURAL TUNNEL.

Tourists travelling South from Route 25 from Cincinnati, Ohio, turn left on Route 25-E at Corbin, Ky., to Cumberland Gap, Va., and take Route 58 to Jonesville, following that Route to Duffield, Virginia, and there connecting with Route 23, only 5 miles from Natural Tunnel.

☆ ☆ ☆

Abingdon, Va. ...57 Miles	Johnson City, Tenn. ...47 Miles
Asheville, N. C. ...125 Miles	Kingsport, Tenn. ...22 Miles
Atlanta, Ga. ...312 Miles	Knoxville, Tenn. ...115 Miles
Big Stone Gap, Va. ...22 Miles	Memphis, Tenn. ...555 Miles
Birmingham, Ala. ...381 Miles	Miami, Fla. ...905 Miles
Bristol, Va.-Tenn. ...44 Miles	Middlesboro, Ky. ...70 Miles
Chattanooga, Tenn. ...253 Miles	Nashville, Tenn. ...309 Miles
Detroit, Mich. ...626 Miles	New Orleans, La. ...744 Miles
Elizabethton, Tenn. ...54 Miles	Newton, Va. ...40 Miles
Erwin, Tenn. ...64 Miles	Pikeville, Ky. ...100 Miles
Gate City, Va. ...16 Miles	Roanoke, Va. ...204 Miles
Greenville, Tenn. ...35 Miles	St. Louis, Mo. ...614 Miles
Greenville, S. C. ...180 Miles	Winst'n-Sa'm, N.C ...584 Miles

Figure 92. Now you could "get there from here." A portion of a circa-1950 brochure for the NTC&CC is quick to point out how easy it was to reach the Tunnel, though the children of the '50s and '60s who traveled these roads in the backseat are likely still suffering motion sickness.

the great cities of Michigan and Ohio to the many resorts and tourist havens of the Eastern Seaboard" (see Figure 92). While the route may, indeed, have been the shortest, it was by no means the straightest, and many of us are still carsick from riding in the back of the old station wagon on U.S. Highway 23.

But probably the mainstay of the property was—and still is—the local population. They had always loved the Tunnel; it was their claim to fame and it was in their backyard. Besides the grounds, where family, church, and group picnics and outings were held, the new lodge also had a meeting room—perhaps the only one between Gate City and Big Stone Gap. The legend of Lover's Leap inspired many a local lovesick couple to share their vows on Table Rock, minus the jump, of course.

The restaurant (see Figure 93) was there, too, but

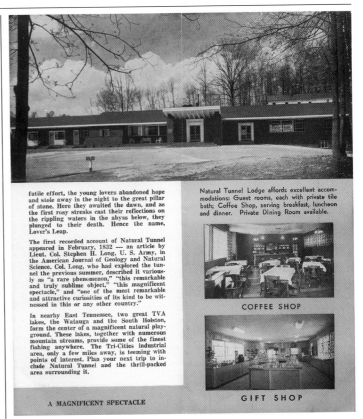

futile effort, the young lovers abandoned hope and stole away in the night to the great pillar of stone. Here they awaited the dawn, and as the first rosy streaks cast their reflections on the rippling waters in the abyss below, they plunged to their death. Hence the name, Lover's Leap.

The first recorded account of Natural Tunnel appeared in February, 1832 — an article by Lieut. Col. Stephen H. Long, U. S. Army, in the American Journal of Geology and Natural Science. Col. Long, who had explored the tunnel the previous summer, described it variously as "a rare phenomenon," "this remarkable and truly sublime object," "this magnificent spectacle," and "one of the most remarkable and attractive curiosities of its kind to be witnessed in this or any other country."

In nearby East Tennessee, two great TVA lakes, the Watauga and the South Holston, form the center of a magnificent natural playground. These lakes, together with numerous mountain streams, provide some of the finest fishing anywhere. The Tri-Cities industrial area, only a few miles away, is teeming with points of interest. Plan your next trip to include Natural Tunnel and the thrill-packed area surrounding it.

A MAGNIFICENT SPECTACLE

Natural Tunnel Lodge affords excellent accommodations: Guest rooms, each with private tile bath; Coffee Shop, serving breakfast, luncheon and dinner. Private Dining Room available.

COFFEE SHOP

GIFT SHOP

Figure 93. A portion of an NTC&CC brochure, circa 1960.

it does not appear to have been frequented as much by the locals. Gil Bledsoe, later to be first park manager, tells of his shock as a young man returning home from military service and paying 75 cents for a hamburger, the same price as admission in 1947! A lucky few, though, could afford that hamburger (see Figure 94).

The gift shop (see Figure 95) was much improved from the NT&CC days. In addition to standard tourist items, the shop carried higher-quality items such as pottery, woodcrafts, and glassware.

It is interesting to note that many of these so-called "kitsch" items sold by tourist attractions in the 1950s through the 1970s—the ones our mothers

Stock Creek Gorge

Natural Tunnel State Park photos
by Ken Murray and Tony Scales

Marshall Spears photos

Four seasons of Natural Tunnel

Natural Tunnel, Chasm & Caverns Corp.

COMPLIMENTARY SEASON PASS

NOT TRANSFERABLE
SUBJECT TO CONDITIONS
ON BACK

1954

Issued To

Mr H H Necessary + Party

By H Y Shanks

Natural Tunnel of Virginia

N⁰ 1224

It is understood and agreed that this pass to The Natural Tunnel, Chasm & Caverns is non-transferable and will be accepted only for the person in whose name it is issued, and that the gate-keeper and other officers of the company will have the right to request identification of the party presenting this pass, and should it be presented by any other than the party to whom issued it will be subject to immediate surrender and cancellation. The person accepting this pass assumes all risk of accidents.

I agree to the above conditions:

Signature _____

Address _____

Occupation _____

Figure 94. In 1954, Mr. Necessary and party were lucky—they received a complimentary season pass signed by manager Hugh Shanks himself; perhaps with the money saved, they could afford to eat at the restaraunt. Woe be to the person fraudulently using the pass, however, as noted by the wording on the reverse side.

Gift Shop - Natural Tunnel, Va.   3-C-157

Figure 95. The Natural Tunnel gift shop, as recorded by a W. W. Cline Company postcard, circa 1950. The W. W. Cline Company's photographs from this era, identifiable by the "C" in the numbering system at lower right, were in stark black-and-white and presented the Tunnel and its surroundings in an almost film noir mood.

Figure 97. My favorite piece, absolutely not for sale. (Photograph by Leslie Bright)

Figure 96. Mementos from the Natural Tunnel gift shop. From left to right: a cedar box filled with marbles, a faux corncob pipe, a brass wall decoration, a pennant (which would have been tied to a car's radio antenna), a cedar jewelry box inscribed "Mother," a saucer with the state of Virginia imprint, a cedar card holder, a brass horse, an ashtray in the shape of Virginia, a "two bears in a swing" salt shaker, two matching, hand-painted flower vases, and a creamer. These knickknacks, originally looked on with some disdain as junk, can now command high prices among collectors. (Photograph by Bob VanGundy)

Figure 98. At last, after miles of winding road, the entrance to Natural Tunnel.

Figure 99. Only 800 feet to go to "Nature's Marvel in Stone."

Figure 100. Your safety is assured.

told us, "Put it back, it's trashy"—are now avidly collected and often sell for much more than their original price (see Figures 96 and 97). The same is true of postcards (see Figures 98-105).

For nearly 30 years, the NTC&CC idled along, never going broke but never getting rich, either. It was essentially a break-even proposition. The locals loved it, had always loved it, and likely will always love it. Employees tell of repeat visitors from other states, coming back year after year. The *Gate City Herald*

proudly reproduced the states and foreign countries listed in the guestbook kept at the lodge. There was always the accidental one-time visitor, drawn by the billboards and brochures. But it just wasn't enough. Attendance never really grew, and of course, overhead always grows. Natural Tunnel, once the "Eighth Wonder of the World," had become to the motoring public just another roadside attraction.

In January 1966, the directors and stockholders of the NTC&CC adopted a resolution to sell, for the

Figure 101. This postcard, a drawing of the Natural Tunnel Lodge, seems to indicate mountains to the horizon, when in actuality there was a spur of Purchase Ridge just behind that precluded a view of the neighboring knobs.

Figure 102. The scene in this Lover's Leap postcard could have come from a fence painter's dream.

Figure 103. The Eagle's Nest. Whenever visiting this spot, I always recall my Great Aunt Flossie's first view from here, clutching her heart with one hand and her niece with another, and gasping, "Why, Nellie!"

Figure 104. A view of the Little Tunnel as recorded by the W. W. Cline Company.

sum of $10, their property—lock, stock, and barrel—that property to serve as the nucleus of a new state park. In January 1967, the Commonwealth formally took possession.

No one is quite clear why the directors got rid of the property. Jack Quillen, son of Belt Quillen, states that the reason is because the company could never raise enough capital for advertising, and without advertising, you simply could not draw an increasing tourist base. Some say they sold the property because of a thing that happens to many jointly owned businesses—the original owners retire or pass away, the next generation loses interest, and the original impetus is lost. All lives, human or business, have their season. The season of private ownership of Natural Tunnel had passed.

SIDE ROOM

In 1940, the Natural Tunnel, Chasm and Caverns Corporation, in conjunction with the *Gate City Herald,* promoted a contest to name the new lodge at Natural Tunnel. Out of over 500 entries from 26 states, with such suggestions as Discovery Trail Lodge, Enchanted Virgin Lodge, Moonshine Lodge, Moonlight Lodge, Magic Chasm Lodge, Magic Tree Lodge, Crater Rim Lodge, and Lost River Lodge, the officers of the company settled on a surprising choice—Natural Tunnel Lodge. Mrs. R. J. Carter of Clinchport, Virginia, won the $5 prize, said the judges, for two reasons: "first, a name carrying out the Tunnel idea and, as Mrs. Carter pointed out, an idea eliminating the necessity of re-educating the public to the natural beauty of the Tunnel and its surroundings."

Not to waste a good pool, the judges decided

Looking down into Natural Tunnel, Va.

Figure 105. Always impressive, whether in color or black-and-white.

to use the five runner-up names—Indians' Tryst, Wee Tunnel Inn, Sun Valley Lodge, Winfield Scott Lodge, and Nantahala—for the cottages, which, as it turned out, were never built.

FREE AGAIN

NATURAL TUNNEL STATE PARK, 1968 TO PRESENT

To protect, preserve and interpret the Commonwealth's greatest phenomenon and its surroundings, and to provide economical and enjoyable recreational experiences for Virginians and their guests.

—1982 internal fact sheet on the purpose, history, and future plans of Natural Tunnel State Park

f the key to real estate is "location, location, location," the key to a state park is "infrastructure, infrastructure, infrastructure." In 1967, the Commonwealth of Virginia inherited a worn-out motel, a stone lavatory, an old gift shop, miles of fencing, and a pole barn. The original master plan for development of the property included a gift shop and cafeteria, to be located at the base of Lover's Leap (not likely, not enough room)—where if you tried hard enough, you could jump from one side of Stock Creek to the other—and a glass elevator from Lover's Leap to that gift shop! But the key to obtaining infrastructure in any government procurement system is "ask for the moon," or in this case, a glass elevator, and then take what you can get.

First, the park staff worked with what they had. The old lodge became the first visitors center, with displays on railroad, Native American, and pioneer history (see Figure 106). Down came the wooden fences, up went the wire ones. New trails were constructed and old ones improved (see Figure 107). Any vestige of the public-address system was removed. (Hooray!) In May of 1971, Natural Tunnel State Park (NTSP) officially opened, and by year's end, 17,600 people had visited the Commonwealth's latest park.

Figure 106. The old Natural Tunnel Lodge was converted into the visitors center and museum when Natural Tunnel State Park opened in 1971. (From the files of Natural Tunnel State Park)

For visitors to Virginia's newest state park, the Tunnel experience was the same as in the days when it was a private operation, except for one important thing—now it was free. You still had to have a bit of oomph to walk the Tunnel Trail—not so bad going down, but a pull coming out.

In those days, you could still walk through the Little Tunnel, cross the plate girder, and then walk through the main attraction, still the greatest of Tunnel experiences, especially for those with vertigo who shy away from the overlooks. The railroad, based on safety concerns, later stopped all foot traffic through the Tunnel, a sad loss. For a few years, the experience of standing in the middle of the Tunnel in twilight, thinking of the forces that caused such an underground expanse to form, was lost to the Tunnel admirer.

But people always want a little more, and it is the duty, and mandate, of a park system to supply it (provided the funds are available, of course). The old NTC&CC knew people wanted to stay at the Tunnel, so they built the lodge, but it in itself was limiting with so few rooms. In 1974, the campground (see Figure 108) opened, an instant success. Now the park could accommodate both the day and the overnight visitor.

With more infrastructure needed, more land was needed. Starting out with the original 144 acres from the old NTC&CC in 1967, various acquisitions and

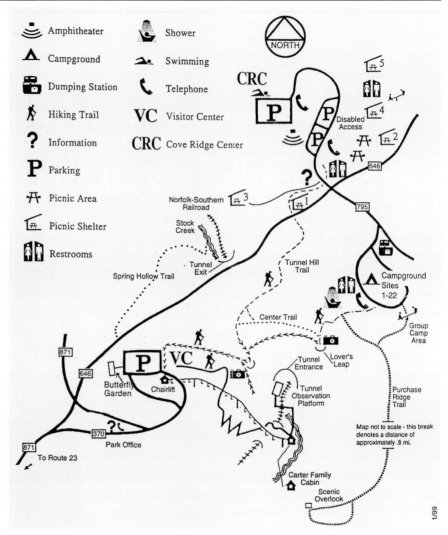

Figure 107. Plan view and trail map for Natural Tunnel State Park. (From the files of Natural Tunnel State Park)

donations have spread the park to its present 850+ acres, with surely more to come. Probably the most interesting addition to the park—other than the Tunnel itself, of course—was the old Natural Tunnel Stone Quarry at Glenita, donated by the heirs of E. H. Walker in 1988, making Natural Tunnel State Park probably the only park in the nation with a quarry!

Figure 108. The campground can service both the wheeled set and traditional tent campers. (Photograph by Leslie Bright)

Figure 109. Plenty of room to spread out the picnic basket in the picnic area. The amphitheater can be seen at the right below the parking area. (Photograph by Leslie Bright)

People like to picnic; in 1975, the rudiments of the picnic area were built, expanded many times since (see Figure 109). People like to swim; in 1983, the pool and concession area was built (see Figure 110). People like to be entertained; in 1986, an amphitheater—the wooden, not stone, kind—was built adjacent to the picnic area, to serve as a stage for music and other audience presentations (see Figure 111). Also at that time, a new park office (see Figure 112) and maintenance shop were constructed.

People like to learn; in 1987, the old lodge was demolished and the present visitors center (see Figure 113) was erected in its place, with improved displays and audiovisual facilities. Because of its remote location far from major city lights, the park has always been a favorite of amateur astronomers, and in 1999, a gazebo (see Figure 114) was built as a locus for stargazing.

And people want to see the Tunnel, which was never easy to get to, so in 1989 a chair lift (see Fig-

ure 115) was constructed, with the help of a helicopter to seat pylons on the steep terrain. When proposed, the idea of a chair lift, an amusement-park-type amenity, caused concern among old friends of the park, but its location south and below the Eagle's Nest—that is, not visible from the South Portal—waylaid those concerns. This conveyance has allowed access to the South Portal for the aged and infirm, greatly increasing visitation. Though diehard Tunnel fans still walk the trail down, they are not shy about riding the chair lift out!

In 1991 a boardwalk was constructed, connecting the chair lift terminus with the South Portal viewing area. This boardwalk includes a bridge crossing of Stock Creek just east of the plate girder, and a pedestrian crossing of the railroad tracks (supported in part by a donation by the Norfolk Southern Railway), complete with warning bells and lights—a favorite of railroad fans and children alike (see Figure 116).

Figure 110. The pool area with Cove Ridge Center in the background. The concession stand is located at the pool entrance. (From the files of Natural Tunnel State Park)

Figure 112. The office at the park entrance. (Photograph by Ken Murray)

Figure 111. The amphitheater serves as the center for music and other performances. (Photograph by Leslie Bright)

Figure 113. The old lodge was torn down and the new visitors center erected in 1987, with displays, a gift shop, and bathroom facilities. The upper chair-lift building is just to the right of this view. (Photograph by Ken Murray)

Figure 114. Because of its remote location, Natural Tunnel State Park is an ideal place for amateur astronomy. This gazebo was constructed on a high point of Cove Ridge north of the picnic area to serve stargazers. (Photograph by Leslie Bright)

In 1997, the park began offering wild cave tours at Bowlin Cave, returning that feature to the Tunnel experience. Natural Tunnel Caverns are also part of the wild caving program. In that year, canoe excursions on the Clinch River joined the outdoor adventure program. And friends of the Tunnel let out a cheer of recovered joy when, in 2003, they once more were able to stand inside the marvel. An adventure trip entitled "Stock Creek Passage" was begun, whereby hardy visitors could visit the interior of the Tunnel by wading Stock Creek, at low water of course, into the North Portal, away from the danger of train traffic.

Keeping with the theme of pioneer heritage, in 1998 NTSP placed the Carter Cabin (see Figure 117) on the old SA&O line east of Stock Creek. This home is believed to have been built of logs originally in the Carter Fort House in nearby Rye Cove. Sometime after 1784, Joseph Carter moved these logs from the fort to construct his home in the Carter Town area of Rye Cove.

A bridge crossing of Stock Creek (see Figure 118), connecting the chair-lift terminus to the old railroad grade, was completed the following year.

In 2003, the Daniel Boone Wilderness Trail Association, in cooperation with Natural Tunnel State Park, constructed a replica of the Anderson Blockhouse, originally built by Captain John Anderson in 1775 in the East Carters Valley region of Scott County, near Wadlow Gap. This fort was the last station travelers on the old Wilderness Trail saw before entering Indian country. Fittingly, the replica (see Figure 119) stands next to the old Fincastle Road, another important historical route, near the park's picnic area.

Natural Tunnel State Park (and indeed, all parks within the Virginia system) promotes environmental education and conservation. To further this goal, in

Figure 115. For the aged or infirm—or the just plain lazy—the valley of Stock Creek can now be reached by chair lift. This view is looking down from the pylon structure, with the Tunnel Trail and lower chair-lift building below. (Photograph by Stewart Scales)

Figure 116. The pedestrian crossing of the railroad tracks at the South Portal, with warning lights and bells. (Photograph by Stewart Scales)

Figure 117. The old Carter Cabin, originally built pre-1784, was moved from Rye Cove to the abandoned SA&O line on the east side of Stock Creek in 1998.

Figure 118. This bridge over Stock Creek connects the lower chair-lift building and the Tunnel Trail to the old SA&O line and the Carter Cabin.

1997, construction was started on the Cove Ridge Education Center, a meeting, classroom, and dormitory complex, adjacent to the pool and concession area. Tragically, only three weeks before opening in August of 1998, this beautiful wood building burned to the ground, for reasons yet unexplained. The park and its friends were deeply hurt by this calamity. Fortunately, it was possible to rebuild the structure (see Figure 120), which finally opened in August of 1999. The building serves as the conference, education, and outdoor-program center for the park.

Fittingly, NTSP is moving toward the goals of the former owners, albeit on a not-for-profit basis. Something is working right; in 2001 the park welcomed over 200,000 visitors, a hundredfold increase from 1938 and a tenfold increase from the park's opening year. Future projects include cabins, more campgrounds, and other additions. And fulfilling the intentions of the old SA&O, later the wishes of the NTC&CC, the Tunnel (the South Portal and Amphitheater) was finally electrified in 1997 with the install-

lation of a lighting system. Fortunately, there are no plans to reinstall a public-address system!

SIDE TRAILS

In 2001, Virginia's park system was recognized for excellence in park management and became the National Gold Medal and State Park Award winner, an award presented by the National Sporting Goods Association's Sports Foundation, Inc., in cooperation with the National Recreation and Park Association. Any visitor will see that Natural Tunnel State Park played no small role in that award, a combination of both the natural wonder it protects and the people who watch over it. One of those people, Saundra Tomlinson, besides being "sweeter 'n punkin' pie," was the first female ranger in the Virginia park system.

Before the advent of the chair lift, it was a short walk down to the Tunnel but always a long walk back. But many a railfan would make that trip for

Figure 119. This replica of the Anderson Blockhouse was constructed by the Daniel Boone Wilderness Trail Association in 2003. Fittingly, it overlooks the old Fincastle Road and Rye Cove.

Figure 120. The Cove Ridge Education Center serves as the educational center for the park. To the right of this view are two dormitories, appropriately named "Clinch" and "Powell." (Photograph by Leslie Bright)

the chance to take the classic photograph of a Norfolk Southern engine emerging from the South Portal and/or the Little Tunnel. The question visitors probably most frequently ask is, "How often do the trains come through?" Of course, the answer is, "Only the dispatcher knows."

This question no doubt ran repeatedly through the minds of two gentlemen who had traveled down from Michigan for the sole purpose of getting that shot, long before the chair lift was thought of. In a pouring rain, they trudged down to the Tunnel and sat for the better part of the afternoon, cameras diligently protected under their ponchos, water dripping off their hoods. With the light fading and no letup of the rain in sight, and not a train to be seen, the men resigned themselves to the lost opportunity, packed up their gear, and started up the trail. Three-quarters of the way up—and certainly too far to run back to catch the moment—they heard that mournful whistle blow. . . .

LEGENDS AND LIES

NOTES AND LOOSE ENDS REGARDING NATURAL TUNNEL

It is the intent of this book to provide a factual history of Natural Tunnel, to support contentions with solid references, and to phrase suppositions clearly where no concrete data exist to support them. Debunking legends and revealing lies is a risky business. Legends are often held closer to the heart, and revealing them is often perceived as a threat. So let's just say that the jury is still out on a few points.

There is a confusing mix, as regards Natural Tunnel, of William Jennings Bryan (the Great Commoner) and Theodore Roosevelt (the Rough Rider). Starting with the Natural Tunnel and Caverns Corporation, the statement that Natural Tunnel is "the eighth wonder of the world" has been attributed to Bryan (see Figure 121), and it is repeated again and again throughout the history of the Tunnel (even on a prominent display in the park's visitors center).

Similarly, the Natural Tunnel State Park files hold pictures of a bannered train, looking suspiciously like the old SA&O seen in so many early postcards, that someone has labeled "Theodore Roosevelt and Party," though no source is attributed and no one knows where the photographs came from. One interviewee stated they were included in a privately pub-

Figure 121. The Great Commoner, William Jennings Bryan, is generally credited with calling Natural Tunnel the "Eighth Wonder of the World." (From the files of Natural Tunnel State Park)

lished collection of old photographs by one Carl Collins of Appalachia, Virginia, but this collection has not been found. A picture in these files has an arrow pointing to a man, standing with a group at the North Portal, labeled "Theodore Roosevelt" (see Figure 122), but this gentleman does not have the stout "bull moose" figure of Roosevelt.

Most passing references to the Tunnel say that the "eighth wonder" quote is Bryan's, but a few say it is Roosevelt's. (By the by, local legend in Burney, California, also has Teddy proclaiming McArthur-Burney Falls, now a state park, the same thing.) The September 18, 1941, issue of the *Gate City Herald* has this to say of the great men who had visited the Tunnel and uttered words of praise: "the late William Jennings Bryan's statement the tunnel was the eighth wonder of the world, as well as numerous similar praises by nationally noted men including the late Theodore Roosevelt."

The July 1, 1956, Centennial Edition of the *Bristol Herald Courier/Virginia-Tennessean* reports, "Theodore Roosevelt spent much time in the area gathering material for his history, *The Winning of the West*. William Jennings Bryan, viewing the spectacle, exclaimed: 'This should be called the Eighth Wonder of the World.'"

Figure 122. This enlargement of a portion of Figure 39 shows a gentleman who resembles Theodore Roosevelt, sometimes credited with calling Natural Tunnel the "Eighth Wonder of the World." The man in the photograph is more likely a railroad official on an SA&O excursion train or the beribboned first regular passenger train from Bristol to Big Stone Gap shown in Figure 31. Additionally, with an ego as big as his smile, Teddy tended to stand in front of, not with, the crowd.

All that can be said about it is that somebody said it. By no means has an exhaustive search been performed to find the source of this quote, but you would think that if one of these distinguished gentlemen had deigned to visit the area, prominent record would exist. None, as yet, has been found. Certainly Bryan and Roosevelt were crisscrossing the country just after the railroad opened, and the Natural Tunnel Route would have been a trip of choice between the Carolinas and Tennessee Valley, and the Midwest. Roosevelt was friends with two of the great political families of Southwest Virginia, those of Auburn L. Pridemore and Campbell Slemp (son of C. Bascom). And Big Stone Gap author John Fox, Jr., had visited the White House and served as a newspaper correspondent with the Rough Riders, and was admired by Roosevelt as a writer of "the strenuous life." However, if you take bets on the source of the quote, choose Bryan. Teddy probably would have simply said, "Bully!"

But one Roosevelt likely visited—and one definitely visited—the Tunnel. In 1908, Franklin Delano Roosevelt, a recent graduate of Harvard, journeyed to the Kentucky and Virginia coalfields for his uncle, Warren Delano. Delano was involved with the growing Virginia Iron, Coal and Coke Company, and Franklin was researching title abstracts for land purchases. His travels conceivably put him on the Natural Tunnel Route.

On July 3, 1941, Franklin's wife, Eleanor, whose father, Elliott Roosevelt, resided in Abingdon in the late 1800s (Teddy was his brother, which makes one wonder if perhaps Elliot could be attributed with the saying), visited the Tunnel for a brief stop while traveling from Ashland, Kentucky, to Asheville, North Carolina, on vacation. A hurried call from the Tunnel to Gate City resulted in an impromptu gathering of citizens at the courthouse of that town to glimpse the First Lady.

In an article on the happening, the *Gate City Herald* reported, in not quite happy terms, "Although not positively identified one of the two women in the car driven by Mrs. Roosevelt was believed to have been her secretary, Mrs. Malvina R. Schneider. The identity of the other woman was not known as the party did not make a definite stop, although it acknowledged greeting from the streets."

A tourist brochure for the Natural Tunnel, Chasm and Caverns Corporation has the following enigmatic statement: "Moving picture producers have traveled across the continent to stage rare scenes here and the Natural Tunnel, unnamed, has thrilled many audiences of the silent screen." Unnamed, indeed; no record of the Tunnel's "moving picture" role has, as yet, been found.

A minor story—that is, one certainly not of the magnitude, renown, and persistence of Poor Dotson/Dodson/Horton—has to do with a preacher riding his horse over the Tunnel, just after the close of the Civil War. It would seem that this preacher

(Professor Fugate, quoted in Robert Addington's *History of Scott County Virginia,* gives the name Reverend H. C. Neal, though I have also heard him called Dotson and Horton!), having ministered to his flock on his Scott County circuit, was returning home when he determined to "take the view."

Riding west down the ridge, he turned his horse east into the woods, planning to ride a short distance, tie his horse, and walk to the edge of the Amphitheater. But due to the thick brush, he rode farther than he planned, when he felt his horse slipping—nowadays we would call it a "four-wheel slide"—down the slope toward the sheer cliff, the ground damp from a previous rain. Closer and closer he slipped, the horse falling on its rear haunches, until Providence intervened and the slide stopped, with the preacher able to look over the horse's bowed head straight down to Stock Creek hundreds of feet below.

After scrambling off and up, and somehow turning the horse, the preacher swooned for a while—a requisite, it would seem, for those who approach the tunnel from above! Returning (carefully this time) to the scene, he discovered that the horse's slide was arrested by a mere protuberance of flint jutting from the rock.

There is probably no cliff, sheer wall, or high spot in the United States (or the world, for that matter) that is not associated with a story of two lovers, denied each other, plummeting to their deaths. The reason this type of story is so popular probably relates to most people's wariness, if not fear, of falling, and falling to their death; romanticizing the fear takes some of it away.

In 1871, Pollard codified this love story for Natural Tunnel, telling the tale of Masoa, a Wyandot (never mind that this tribe lived in the Upper Ohio

Valley) maiden. Denied her lover and promised by her father to a neighboring chief, on the day of her betrothal, the lover and maiden climbed to the heights of Lover's Leap to proclaim their love to the irate wedding party in the gorge below. A well-placed arrow, an amazing shot from 400 feet below, from the jilted chief kills the lover, who Masoa clutches to her breast as she leaps, falling in a lover's embrace at the foot of the murdering chief, who is promptly tomahawked by Masoa's brother.

This tale came to play an important role in the Natural Tunnel and Caverns Corporation's, (later the Natural Tunnel, Chasm and Caverns Corporation) promotion of Lover's Leap, making the story one of intertribal (Cherokee and Shawnee, closer to reality) taboo. The story was put into book form by Clara Talton Fugate, who again makes it an intertribal affair, with the Sac/Fox maiden Winnoa (never mind that the Sac/Fox Tribe was from the northeast, later the Ohio Valley) denied her true love, Swift Foot. The story ends as a simple double suicide.

There is, of course, no way to test the veracity or provenance of this tale and its many variations. One interviewee summed his regard of the story this way: "Can't be true. I can see pushing a woman off the cliff, but I'd be danged if I'd go with her."

There are at least two real stories of death at the Tunnel. A visitor climbing up the Tunnel trail sometime in the 1940s or 1950s suffered a heart attack and died. A door from the gift shop was removed and used as a litter to carry the body out. During World War II, a man rode to the Tunnel on the Tri-State Bus (serving Tennessee, Virginia, and Kentucky), got off, and walked to the Tunnel Overlook. There, it is reported, he removed his jacket, folded it neatly, and put it on the ground. He then placed a woman's watch on top of the jacket, climbed the fence, and leaped to his death.

The Tunnel, perhaps because of its overpowering presence, tends to make the human mind exaggerate. Probably the best tale to date is the claim by one Ralph Dickenson, who in 1931 flew from his home in California to visit family in Southwest Virginia. He sent a card to a friend in Bristol, Virginia, which made its way into the local newspapers due to the claims made thereon.

Mr. Dickenson wrote: "Flew right through this tunnel while following the railroad in the rain. Never touched the sides. Have the record of being first man in the United State to fly a plane underground." This statement prompted W. H. Wren, Sr., a pilot living in Big Stone Gap, to point out to the papers that Mr. Dickenson's plane, a Stinson Detroiter cabin craft, had a wingspan of 41 feet, 8 inches, whereas portions of the Tunnel would barely admit an 18-foot-wide train!

And of course, it is fairly common knowledge that Natural Tunnel is not natural at all, but rather is the result of excavation by one Johnathan Swift, who in his search for silver. . . .

Editor's note: The legend of Johnathan Swift and his lost silver mine is popular throughout the Southern Appalachian Mountains.

THE GEOLOGY OF NATURAL TUNNEL
A TALE OF WATER, STONE, AND TIME

THERE IS A PLACE WHERE DEEP TIME DWELLS, ON RIDGES BLUE, IN VALLEY DELLS. . . . / OF LIME, OF COAL, OF WATERS SALT, FOLDED STONE AND THRUSTING FAULT. . . . / PLATEAUS OF PINE, MOUNTS OF FIR, LEAVES IN STONE AND BONES ENDURE. . . . / TO KNOW THIS PLACE, THIS SCHEME, THIS LAND, TURN TO THOUGHTS OF EARTH AT HAND. . . ."

—ANTHONY S. SCALES, 1998
FROM "LOST FRANKLIN"

SO HOW MUCH DYNAMITE DID IT TAKE TO MAKE THAT TUNNEL?

—QUERY TO THE AUTHOR BY A VISITOR ON A TOUR OF NATURAL TUNNEL, 1994

ven though the word *natural* precedes the word *tunnel* in the name of this place, some still find it difficult to grasp that the Tunnel could have formed by any means other than high explosives. Perhaps this doubt generates from the overwhelming presence of the railroad and the difficulty of seeing beyond the human life-span.

I remember an report by a local television station, in conjunction with the dedication of the chair-lift facility, when the interviewer asked me the inevitable question, "Could you explain to our viewers how Natural Tunnel formed?"

I launched into a practiced discourse on how the Tunnel was created, but after about three minutes, I noticed that both the reporter and the cameraman were rolling their eyes and stifling yawns. When I finished, the interviewer came back to life and asked, "Could you *briefly* sum up the formation of Natural Tunnel?"

Grasping for an answer, I said, "If you give Mother Nature enough time, water can make a big hole in the ground." That statement, of course, was the five-second sound and video bite used for the broadcast.

Brevity may make for a quick bite, but there is little satisfaction without the meal. To understand how the Tunnel came to be, we need a full-course dinner, enjoyed one bite at a time.

WHERE ARE WE?

To coin, or rather to steal, a phrase, "Natural Tunnel can be reached by a pleasant drive over good roads, from many points" (see Figures 57, 123, and 124). Natural Tunnel is located approximately six

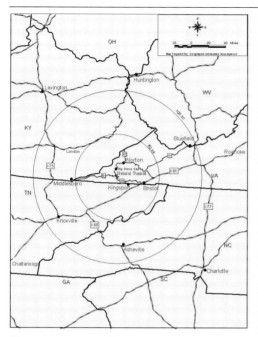

Figure 123. Natural Tunnel is located approximately six miles north of the Virginia/Tennessee border, one mile east of U.S. Route 23/58/421, on Route 871. (Map courtesy of Geographic Information Development)

Figure 124. An aerial view of Natural Tunnel and the surrounding area. The upland karst area of Rye Cove, now predominantly pasture, is shown well here. The area pictured is approximately 36 square miles (6 miles by 6 miles). (Image courtesy of the U. S. Geological Survey)

miles due north of the Virginia/Tennessee border in the western half of Scott County, Virginia. From the nearest "capital road," U.S. Route 23/58/421, access to Natural Tunnel State Park is gained from Route 871 to Route 646. The former road traces, in part, the old Wilderness Road, and the latter intersects the old Fincastle Road at Route 650 and also crosses directly over the Tunnel.

Natural Tunnel is located in the Ridge and Valley Physiographic Province (see Figure 125). A physiographic province is distinct from others based on landforms and geology. For example, if we say "Great Plains Province," immediately the mind conjures up the beautiful flat and rolling spaces of Kansas—we instinctively understand the lay of the land.

The Ridge and Valley Province echoes its name, a series of ridges and mountain ranges and their intervening valleys. Natural Tunnel pierces one of those ridges, Purchase Ridge. The creek that flows through the Tunnel, Stock Creek, is a tributary of the Clinch River, one of the great rivers and the namesake of the region.

Just to the north, the massif of High Knob and Powell Mountain are placed in the Appalachian Plateaus Physiographic Province. While the highest point in Wise County has the appearance of Ridge and Valley topography, it is actually more akin to the coal-bearing rocks that lie in the great coalfields of Southwest Virginia, north of Stone and Little Stone mountains. Natural Tunnel serves as a point of passage for this coal on its journey south and east.

The Blue Ridge Mountains rise to the southeast, in the Blue Ridge Physiographic Province of Virginia, North Carolina, and Tennessee. Crossing these highlands, the early settlers followed the Wilderness Road to the Kentucky bluegrass and points west. That trail, of course, passes by the entrance to Natural Tunnel State Park.

STOCK CREEK

Stock Creek rises on the flanks of Powell Mountain (see Figure 126). Lieutenant Colonel Long stated the stream was so named for the livestock grazing along its reaches (it has also been called Buckeye Branch in the past). From an initial elevation of nearly 3,200 feet above sea level, Stock Creek and its tributaries, Laurel Fork and Dry Fork, drop nearly 1,600 feet southeast to Hunter Valley. Stock Creek then flows southwest, following the trace of the Hunter Valley Fault, until just northeast of Sunbright, where it takes a nearly due south, though meandering, course.

At Sunbright, Stock Creek begins bisecting the highlands; to the southwest, the resultant ridge is called Purchase Ridge, and to the northeast, Cove Ridge. At the North Portal (see Figures 127 and 128), Stock Creek has fallen over 1,800 feet to an elevation of approximately 1,390 feet above sea level. Entering the Clinch River at Clinchport, Stock Creek drains 18,633 acres, or slightly over 29 square miles.

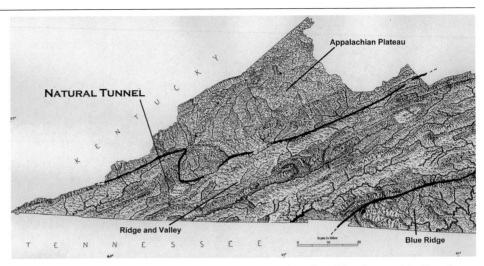

Figure 125. Natural Tunnel lies in the Ridge and Valley Physiographic Province. Stock Creek rises on the flanks of Powell Mountain, north of Natural Tunnel. Powell Mountain lies in the Appalachian Plateau Province. Pioneer travelers from the Blue Ridge Province of North Carolina and Tennessee passed by Natural Tunnel on the Wilderness Road as they made their way across these three great provinces to the Kentucky bluegrass. (A portion of "Physiographic Diagram of Virginia," 1991, by Edgar Bingham, courtesy of the Virginia Division of Mineral Resources)

THE ROCKS

The strata of Purchase Ridge are assigned to the Knox Group, named for exposures near Knoxville, Tennessee. This group of rocks was deposited approximately 500 million years ago, in the Cambrian and Ordovician periods (see Figure 129). At this time, the area where the Knox Group was deposited was a great shallow sea, of warm climate, not unlike the modern Caribbean Sea.

This sea was prolific with invertebrate animals that built their shells from calcium, carbon, and oxygen in these warm waters. These shells, upon death of the animal, became the basis for the formation of limestone—calcium carbonate—along with direct precipitation from the seawater. This limestone sediment reacted with the overlying seawater, and magnesium replaced some of the calcium. The result was calcium-magnesium carbonate, called *dolostone,* the dominant rock type within the Knox Group. Dolostone is composed of the mineral *dolomite;* sometimes dolostone is referred to informally as "dolomite." Collectively, limestone and dolostone are referred to as *carbonates.*

Many of the carbonate beds within the Knox Group contain significant amounts of sand, and some sandstone beds are present. This indicates that sand was deposited into this shallow sea from a nearby continent or island and was then incorporated into the carbonate sediment.

Strata in the area also contain abundant chert, which is fine-grained silica (silicon dioxide). It likely originated from the accumulation of silica from dead organisms, such as the shells of diatoms and sponge spicules (which formed the skeletal framework of the sponge). Some of this chert may have also originated from volcanic ash, as there is evidence of volcanic ash beds within the Knox Group. The trails and slopes within NTSP are abundantly covered with chert (see Figure 130). Chert is much more resistant to erosion and dissolution than dolostone.

Unfortunately, few fossils are found within the dolostone in the park, likely due to dissolution of the original shells and conversion of the limestone to dolostone. Fossilized laminations of algae are common, however, giving the dolostone a wavy appearance (see Figure 131). These algal mats formed in very shallow waters of the ancient sea. When exposed, the blue-green algae desiccated and died and were then covered with more layers of carbonate sediment. Then a new mat would grow, and the process would repeat.

Similarly, the algae could trap sediment, particularly silt and sand, and still survive, binding the

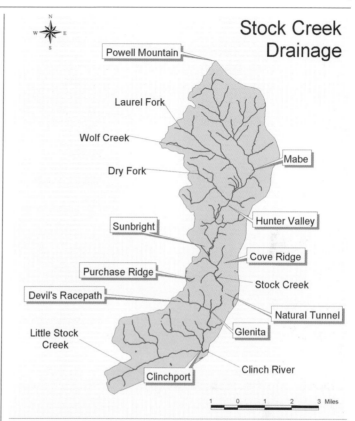

Figure 126. After rising on Powell Mountain, Stock Creek follows Hunter Valley southwest to Horton's Summit (Sunbright), where it turns nearly due south. To the east, the resulting ridge is called Cove Ridge, and to the west, Purchase Ridge. Stock Creek enters the Clinch River at Clinchport. (Map design by Leslie Bright)

sediment and forming layers slightly more resistant to erosion than the overlying and underlying limestone. In places, these repeated algal mats formed softball- to basketball-sized structures called *stromatolites* (see Figure 132).

STRUCTURE IN THE ROCKS

After the Knox Group sediments were deposited, they were buried by overlying formations and underwent compaction and lithification, turning

Figure 127. The Hidden Tunnel and Stock Creek entrance at the North Portal. Prior to the construction of the railroad bed, Stock Creek flowed to the left, toward the entrance to the Hidden Tunnel, and then swept right. In the center of the view is the "pillar" described by Low, resulting from construction of the Hidden Tunnel.

Figure 128. Looking out of the natural stream entrance at the North Portal. The pillar and small solution cavity is just to the right, and the railroad bed retaining wall can be seen in the distance. (Photograph by Leslie Bright)

to stone. Buried thousands of feet deep, the strata lay relatively undisturbed until the Appalachian Orogeny—the event that formed present eastern North America as we know it.

An *orogeny* is a mountain-building event, and the formation of the present-day Appalachians began approximately 300 million years ago. At that time, Proto-Africa (*proto* meaning "that which comes before") and Proto-North America were moving toward each other, driven by the inexorable forces of plate tectonics. Their collision resulted in the uplift of the Appalachian Mountains on the North American continent.

While it is relatively easy to envision that rocks will rise when two land masses collide, it is not so easy to envision what occurs at depth in these rising mountains. With such huge forces, first the rocks at depth will bend, the process of *folding*. With increasing pressure, they bend more, confined by the tremendous weight of overlying (and underlying) rocks. However, as all things have their limits, so do the rocks, and when forces become too great, they do what all things will—they break. Breaks in the rocks along which no movement has occurred are called *fractures*. When movement occurs along a fracture, the fracture becomes a *fault*.

The folding of the rocks in the area of Natural Tunnel resulted in formation of two large synclines, the Rye Cove Syncline and the Purchase Ridge Syncline (see Figure 133). A *syncline* is a downward fold of strata, resulting in a "U" shape. While this shape would seem to promote the formation of valleys, it actually compresses the rocks and makes them more resistant to erosion. Hence, in the southeastern United States, many of our major ridges, mountains, and other upland landforms are synclinal.

EON	ERA	PERIOD/ EPOCH	FORMATION	SYMBOLS ON MAP AND CROSS SECTION	AGE MILLIONS OF YEARS AGO (MA)
PHANEROZOIC	CENOZOIC	HOLO-CENE	✱ Unnamed Alluvial And Colluvial Deposits On Floodplains, In Terraces, And In Fan Deposits	t	
		PLEIS-TOCENE		f	1.6
	PALEOZOIC	MISSISSIPPIAN	Pennington Group		320
			Newman Limestone	Mu	
			Maccrady Formation		
			Grainger Formation		
		DEVONIAN	Chattanooga Shale	Du	360
			Wildcat Valley Sandstone		408
		SILURIAN	Clinch Sandstone, Rose Hill, And Hancock Formations	Su	
					438
		ORDOVICIAN	Numerous Limestone And Shale Formations	Ols	
		CAMBRIAN	✱ Knox Group And Maynardville Limestone	€Od	505
			Nolichucky, Rogersville Shales	€sh	
			Maryville, Rutledge Limestones	€ls	
			Rome And Pumpkin Valley Formations	€ss	
			Shady Dolomite		
			Chilhowee Group		
			Ocoee Series		570
	PROTEROZOIC		Grenville "Basement" ?		1,000
	ARCHE-OZOIC				

✱ Formation exposed at Natural Tunnel.

Figure 129. The major stratigraphic units and geologic time scale for the Natural Tunnel area. Natural Tunnel formed in dolostone of the Knox Group of the Cambro-Ordivician Age, approximately 500 million years ago. (From "The Geology of Natural Tunnel State Park," 1990, by Robert C. Milici, courtesy of the Virginia Division of Minerals Resources)

Figure 130. The dolostone in the vicinity of Natural Tunnel contains abundant chert, such as the cobbles seen here along the Tunnel Hill Trail. Chert is microcrystalline quartz (silicon dioxide) and is highly resistant to weathering. The dolostone dissolves, leaving the chert. If you stumble across a great pile of these in the Ridge and Valley Province, or find them in the shape of a rectangle, it's not due to visitors from Outer Space—it's an old corn patch. (Photograph by Craig Seaver)

Figure 131. The dolostone in the vicinity of Natural Tunnel is mostly devoid of fossils but does display algal laminations, which gives the rock a wavy appearance, such as here at the base of Pylon 2 of the chair lift. (Photograph by Leslie Bright)

Figure 132. Algal laminations sometimes form softball- to basketball-sized structures such as this specimen recovered from the old Natural Tunnel Stone Quarry. (Photograph by Craig Seaver)

IN THE TUNNEL

The straight-line distance through the Tunnel, from the edge of the overhang at the South Portal to the edge of the vertical wall at the North Portal, is 763 feet. Following the curves of the railroad track, the distance is 838 feet. The point at the South Portal where the overhang becomes vertical is approximately 70 feet above Stock Creek.

All along this way, about 20 feet above the stream, the trace of the Glenita Fault can be seen (see Figure 135). The Glenita Fault is actually a zone of numerous small faults, where the individual beds have slid over each other like individual cards in a deck. At the upper boundary of the zone, the bottom of the bed above the zone is *slickensided,* polished smooth and striated by movement along the fault. Below the zone, near stream level, the beds of dolostone are folded into the stream. A normal fault can be seen atop the Glenita Fault above the Saltpeter Cave at the South Portal (see Figure 136).

Approximately 300 feet into the Tunnel from the South Portal is the highest portion of the Tunnel (see Figures 137 and 138). Here, the roof is approximately 35 feet above the railroad bed and 50 feet above the stream. The roof is distinctly circular, or cupola shaped, at this point. In the east wall of the Tunnel, one side of a normal fault can be seen. The trace of this fault can be followed directly into the center of the roof, again pointing to the importance of fracturing that enhanced dissolution. Water can often be found dripping from the roof. At this point, the distance across the Tunnel is approximately 145 feet.

The Glenita Fault—the break in the rocks that connects the Rye Cove and Purchase Ridge synclines—is most important to understanding the formation of Natural Tunnel. The Glenita Fault is a thrust fault, i.e., the strata above the fault have been thrust to the northwest relative to the strata below the fault.

This fault is the key element in the formation of Natural Tunnel. Associated with the Glenita Fault are subsidiary normal faults. A *normal fault* is one in which the rocks above the fault (called the *hanging wall*) have moved downward relative to the rocks below the fault (called the *foot wall*); the angle of the fault is usually 45 to 90 degrees. This type of fault dominates in the Basin and Range Province of the southwestern United States. A normal fault atop the Glenita Fault is well displayed at the old Natural Tunnel Stone Quarry (see Figure 134).

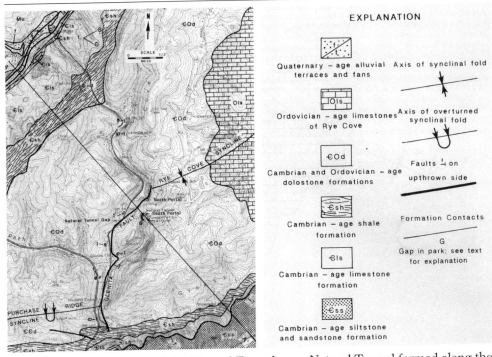

EXPLANATION

Quaternary - age alluvial
terraces and fans

Axis of synclinal fold

Ordovician - age limestones
of Rye Cove

Axis of overturned
synclinal fold

€Od

Cambrian and Ordovician -age
dolostone formations

Faults ⊥ on
upthrown side

€sh

Cambrian - age shale
formation

Formation Contacts

G

Gap in park; see text
for explanation

€ls

Cambrian - age limestone
formation

€ss

Cambrian - age siltstone
and sandstone formation

Figure 133. Geologic map of the Natural Tunnel area. Natural Tunnel formed along the Glenita Fault, a thrust fault connecting two great downward folds of strata, the Rye Cove and Purchase Ridge synclines. The areas designated by a "t" on the map represent stream deposits left by ancestral Stock Creek when it was at higher elevation, before eroding to its present level and before all flow entered the (future) Natural Tunnel. (From "The Geology of Natural Tunnel State Park," 1990, by Robert C. Milici, courtesy of the Virginia Division of Minerals Resources)

feet from the edge of the North Portal, a normal fault is visible. This is the other side of the fault block first seen at the highest point in the Tunnel.

THE NORTH PORTAL

The distance from Stock Creek to the top of the ridge above the North Portal, where State Road 646 crosses the Tunnel, is approximately 250 feet. Unlike the South Portal, the North Portal wall sustains much more vegetation. This north-facing slope of Purchase Ridge does not receive direct sunlight in the winter, remaining wet or frozen, affording vegetation better rooting spots. Like the South Portal, an amphitheater, obscured by vegetation, is present, but on a smaller scale. It is pertinent to note the presence of Canada yew (*Taxus canadensis*, see Figure 140) here and in other nearby shady, cool spots. This northern species is a Pleistocene relict, a leftover from the last ice age, that has found a home long after the periglacial climate has disappeared.

The Hidden Tunnel is reached 550 feet from the South Portal. Here, where Emile Low's two "caverns" intersect, is the greatest width of the Tunnel, nearly 200 feet. In the pillar formed by construction of the Hidden Tunnel, at stream level, is a small cave/solution cavity approximately 30 feet long (see Figure 139). Chert nodules and layers can be seen in the dolostone here and have even formed a small bridge in the cavity. Across the stream from the cave entrance, "fresh" calcite deposits can be seen in the roof above the stream.

Just past the Hidden Tunnel, approximately 150

The upper reaches of the wall here show horizontal layering of the dolostone, but as one looks down to the top of the entrance, the layers are inclined at a high angle east of the entrance and are vertical over the entrance. These layers are above the Glenita Fault, and as such, have moved to the northwest and were dragged along the fault to their present

Figure 134. The Glenita Fault is a thrust fault, with dominant movement to the northwest. Atop the fault, however, normal faulting is present, where principal movement is vertical, such as seen here in the northeast wall of the old Natural Tunnel Stone Quarry. Trace the thick white band of dolostone near the upper third of the wall across the fault, and you will see that the east (right) side of the fault has dropped approximately 5-10 feet. Note also the preferential dissolution (that is, acidic water has preferred to attack the fractured, hence more easily dissolved, surface of the fault) and the widening of the fault surface. The Glenita Fault, which is nearly horizontal here, is just above the zone of alternating dark and light ribbon-banded dolostone in the lower third of the wall. (Photograph by Ken Murray)

Stock Creek flows through a gorge with near-vertical slopes. North of the Tunnel, the valley is wider, and a small alluvial plain is present. This type of valley, formed in karst terrain, is called a *blind* valley. A typical valley widens and opens downstream, but at the North Portal, the valley ends abruptly, causing topographic contours to wrap around at the Tunnel entrance. South of the Tunnel, the gorge is much more constricted, until it widens at the community of Glenita. These near-vertical slopes are maintained by the nature of the rock. Dolostone, while susceptible to dissolution, is a tough rock, one of the reasons it is used for building and road construction.

THE SOUTH PORTAL AND THE AMPHITHEATER

The South Portal and the Amphitheater are the most impressive portions of Natural Tunnel and the most easily observed. As noted

position. The actual fault surface is readily apparent if the vertical beds above and to the right (west) of the entrance are traced down to where they meet the beds inclined slightly to the left (east); the point of contact is the Glenita Fault (see Figure 141).

THE GORGE OF STOCK CREEK

Cutting through Purchase Ridge and Natural Tunnel before entering the Clinch River at Clinchport,

previously, the Glenita Fault is readily seen at the western side of the entrance. The layered strata in the walls, except near the fault, are near horizontal, though those with a keen eye can discern a slight dip northward to the axis of the Rye Cove Syncline.

Unlike the North Portal, the entrance here has a distinct overhang. Also unlike the North Portal, the wall above the South Portal and the walls of the Amphitheater are nearly devoid of vegetation; fac-

Figure 135. The Glenita Fault at the western side of the South Portal. Can you see "Big Tennessee" and "Little Kentucky" (names used by the author to clue visitors in to the location of the Glenita Fault), the two rhombohedra of light-colored rock in the center of the view? Just below "Big Tennessee," note the wider crack; this crack is the upper surface of the Glenita Fault. Note how the dolostone is folded and contorted beneath this fault plane, especially in the lower right of the view.

Figure 136. Just above Saltpeter Cave, the top of the opening almost hidden by the talus pile here, is a normal fault. Note the two whitish lines running from the apex of the opening at 45-degree angles; these mark the edges of the normal fault. Note the folded beds beneath the fault and to the left of the opening. Dissolution of the rock to form Saltpeter Cave was enhanced by this normal fault associated with the Glenita Fault.

ing south, they undergo regular freeze and thaw cycles during the winter, effectively cleaning the wall of any loose debris and preventing the rooting of plants.

To the right (east) of the South Portal, and below the Shelter Caves, a talus slope has formed. *Talus* is rock and soil debris, moving downslope due to gravity, which forms an apron along a ridge or escarpment. The debris here acts as a sponge for water and supports lush vegetation, including spring wildflowers, particularly trillium.

The southwestern terminus of the Amphitheater, the Eagle's Nest (Tunnel Overlook), is approximately 280 feet above Stock Creek. The distance from Stock Creek to the edge of vegetation at the trail directly over the entrance is approximately 350 feet. The southeastern terminus of the Amphi-

theater, at Lover's Leap and the Tower, is approximately 400 feet above Stock Creek. The distance from Stock Creek to the nearest high point on Purchase Ridge, at the park campground, is approximately 550 feet; if the Washington Monument were placed at the South Portal, at the campground you would be even with the top of the monument.

From the Eagle's Nest across the Amphitheater to Lover's Leap is approximately 400 feet. Around the Amphitheater from the Eagle's Nest to Lover's Leap is approximately 1,200 feet; to the Tower, 1,300 feet, or nearly a quarter mile.

FORMATION

The dolostone found in the Natural Tunnel area is inherently impermeable; water cannot pass through it. But obviously water is passing through Purchase

Figure 137. The highest point in Natural Tunnel is 300 feet from the South Portal. Here, the roof is distinctly dome, or cupola, shaped. One side of a normal fault, inclined to the north at approximately 45 degrees, intersects the high point of the roof. Water is often found dripping from the fault at this point.

Figure 138. Facing out of the South Portal. The viewpoint of the previous photograph is where the sun is shining on the railroad bed retaining wall. The talus pile below the Saltpeter Cave is to the right, just past the entrance, at stream level. Always a magnificent view. (Photograph by Leslie Bright)

Figure 139. A small cave/solution cavity, approximately 30 feet long and trending east, is found at stream level in the pillar formed by construction of the Hidden Tunnel. Note the water droplets glistening on the roof, and the debris on the floor from Stock Creek's high waters.

Figure 140. This Canada yew (*Taxus canadensis*), a Pleistocene relict, has found a home along the amphitheater walls of the North Portal, which is in shade most of the year. (Photograph by Bill Cawood)

Ridge, in the form of Stock Creek flowing through Natural Tunnel. How did this happen?

Though the dolostone is impermeable, it will dissolve in acidic water. Most rainwater is weakly acidic, and when it passes through organic material, such as forest litter, it becomes more acidic, principally by the presence of carbonic acid. When an acid combines with a base, such as one of the carbonate rocks, carbon dioxide gas and calcium and magnesium ions in solution are produced. As such, the rock is "lost," simply dissolved and flushed away. This process results in *karst* landforms, with sinkholes, disappearing streams, and, most importantly, cavern formation. Natural Tunnel lies on the western edge of Rye Cove, the largest *karst cove* (a basin formed by the dissolution of carbonate rocks) in Virginia.

Even as early as 1816, Francis Walker Gilmer,

challenging one of Thomas Jefferson's views of the world, recognized that caverns formed by the dissolution of rock. He stated, "This rock is soluble in water to such a degree, as to be found in solution with all the waters of the country, and is so soft as to yield not only to its chemical agency, but also to its mechanical attrition." Though he erred somewhat in believing that some caverns formed in the "original crystallization of the rock," he had the basic facts correct.

Of course, when one stands in front of Natural Tunnel, the sheer immensity begs for more of an explanation than "the rock dissolved away." In 1936, Herbert P. Woodward took up this problem in his paper "Natural Bridge and Natural Tunnel, Virginia," continuing the comparison of the two phenomenons. Woodward postulated that Stock Creek originally flowed southwest through Hunter Valley to Duffield as a tributary of the North Fork of the Clinch River, and that Purchase Ridge was an unbisected highland, with that portion of the ridge south of Natural Tunnel occupied by a "small but vigorous tributary of Clinch River proper."

Woodward thought that at some point in the past, the tributary to the North Fork was diverted to the south through underground channels in the vicinity of Sunbright, thus becoming Stock Creek. In other words, he invoked underground stream piracy of Stock Creek toward karstland forming in the (future) Natural Tunnel area. Stock Creek then entered sinkholes and a cavern system. This cavern was eventually exposed by dissolution and erosion by the "vigorous tributary" and Stock Creek, thus causing cavern collapse. Stock Creek was then able to flow through Purchase Ridge, finding a much shorter route to the local base level—the

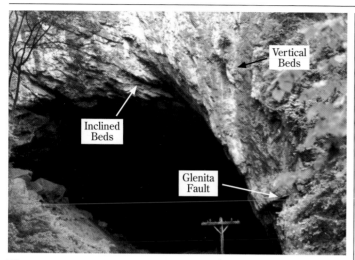

Figure 141. Note that above this telegraph pole at the North Portal, the beds of dolostone are vertical, rolling over to highly inclined to the left of the view. However, note that immediately to the right of the pole, the beds are inclined to the pole; where these gently inclined beds meet the vertical beds is the plane of the Glenita Fault. Movement along the fault was to the northwest (right), and as the beds above the fault moved, they were dragged into their vertical position.

Clinch River—than flowing to the Clinch via the North Fork. Woodward provided a series of diagrams that elegantly portrays this process (see Figure 142).

Interestingly, in 1988, Tony Waltham, a noted British cave researcher, and in 1990, Robert C. Milici, then state geologist of Virginia, came to very similar conclusions on the formation of Natural Tunnel, independent of each other and unknowing of the other's work. Dr. Waltham approached the Natural Tunnel problem from a classic *geomorphologic* context, whereas Dr. Milici employed both a geomorphologic and *structural* scheme. The former interprets the evolution of the present landscape in terms of landform development in relation to the underlying geology, whereas the latter also considers the role of deformation (faulting and folding) on landscape development.

When the geology of Natural Tunnel was first mapped by William B. Brent in 1963, he interpreted the deformation in the dolostone at the South Portal to be *soft-sediment deformation,* that is, slumping and slippage of the carbonate sediment before it became stone. Milici, however, recognized that the folding and deformation within the dolostone occurred after the sediment had turned to rock. Hence, the folding and deformation had to be related to faulting of the rock.

The obvious coincidence that the Tunnel lies along the fault pointed to the fault's control on the Tunnel's formation. Remember, dolostone is impermeable, but it will dissolve, and if the rock is fractured, dissolution of the rock will occur more readily at those fracture surfaces. Acidic water can attack and dissolve the broken surfaces, and can do this as deep as water can circulate along these fractures, below ground level. Most dissolution occurs at the local water table, that is, relatively shallow, usually within tens of feet of the ground/atmosphere contact. These fractures were, and still are, the conduits along which water could move and dissolve the dolostone.

Even though Waltham was unaware of the fault, his interpretation of the origin of Natural Tunnel almost mirrors that of Milici. Both rejected Woodward's cavern-collapse theory, though Waltham (as do I) supports Woodward's theory that Stock Creek originally flowed as a tributary to the North Fork of the Clinch River. Both assert that in the past, Stock Creek flowed over/around the (future) Natural Tunnel when the land surface was at a higher level, before erosion. Milici found evidence of alluvial terrace deposits on the high ground above Stock Creek,

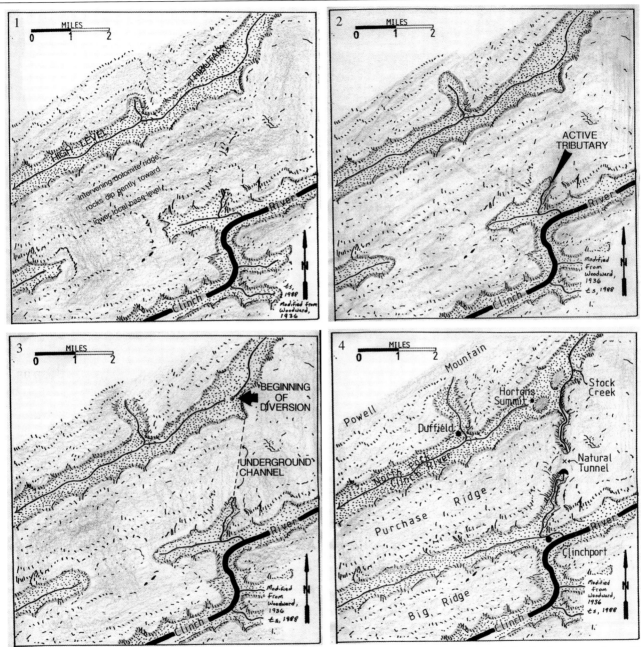

Figure 142. This series of views, modified from Woodward, shows his concept of the evolution of the landscape to form Natural Tunnel. In the first, the North Fork, originating on Powell Mountain, is a high-level tributary of the Clinch River, with an intervening ridge. In the second, Stock Creek begins to erode into the intervening ridge. In the third, karst formation begins to divert some of the flow of the North Fork through a cavern system to Stock Creek. Finally, through continued karst development and ultimately cavern collapse, the headwaters of the North Fork are completely diverted, forming Stock Creek and the Natural Tunnel.

near Tunnel Gap and Glenita Church, proving that the stream once flowed at a higher elevation.

Milici and Waltham also postulated that a *doline,* or sinkhole, formed at the location of the (future) North Portal, and as time passed, more and more water was diverted from Stock Creek into the sinkhole, with the water emerging as a spring at the location of the (future) South Portal. Finally, the entire flow of the stream passed through the Tunnel. Continuing erosion downcut the streambed and the valley of Stock Creek. The former sinkholes at the North and South portals were exposed, revealing their sheer rock walls as the amphitheaters we see today. The former underground passageway for the stream, connecting the two amphitheaters, was left as the Natural Tunnel, which itself continues to degrade by roof breakdown. Milici, following Woodward's lead, provided a series of diagrams to show this progression (see Figure 143).

Can we say how long it took for Natural Tunnel to form? Indeed, dissolution of the rocks is happening right now, but can we state when this process started, and when Natural Tunnel first existed in the form we see it today? Not with any certainty,

but this process definitely took tens, if not hundreds, of thousands of years. It is sometimes possible to ascertain minimum dates of cave formation by paleomagnetic dating of cave sediments, but obviously none are left in Natural Tunnel. Natural Tunnel, from the point when it started as a tiny crack dissolving slowly, is probably on the order of 750,000 to 1,000,000 years old, and has likely stood as we see it today, albeit with the loss of a stone or two, for the past 10,000 years.

Lastly, Milici remarks that, in the earliest part of the process, "ancestral Stock Creek may have plunged over the upper part of the Amphitheater when ancestral Stock Creek stood at a much higher level and when its underground outlet through the tunnel was plugged." His statement would have done the old Natural Tunnel, Chasm and Caverns Corporation proud, for in their tourist brochure, they assert, "Were it possible to turn the flood of Niagara River over the great circular walls of Natural Tunnel, there would be a Niagara Falls nearly twice the height of the present Niagara."

What an attraction we would have if we'd just build a dam across Stock Creek at the North Portal. . . .

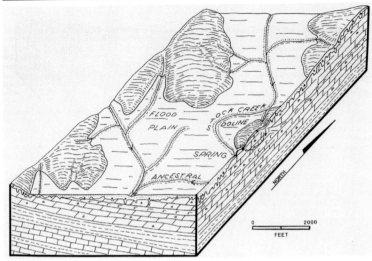

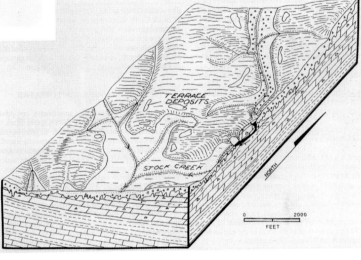

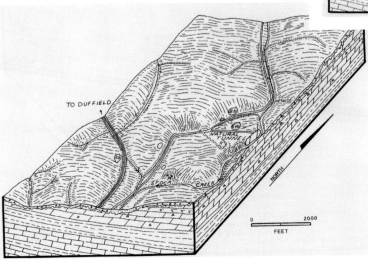

Figure 143. This series of views from Milici shows his concept of the formation of Natural Tunnel. In the first, a portion of Stock Creek is diverted into a doline (sinkhole). In the second, erosion and lowering of the land and continued karst development have caused all of the drainage of Stock Creek to be diverted underground; Stock Creek no longer flows over the (future) Tunnel Gap, but rather resurfaces as a spring at the site of the present South Portal. In the third, with continued downcutting, particularly by the lower reaches of Stock Creek, the former underground passageway is exposed as the Natural Tunnel we see today. (From "The Geology of Natural Tunnel State Park," 1990, by Robert C. Milici. Courtesy of the Virginia Division of Minerals Resources)

EPILOGUE

Geologists are, by and large, a stoic, stolid, and unexcitable lot. We don't worry too much about global warming, it's happened before, or extinctions, they've happened before, or floods (except where we build our houses), they've happened before . . . well, you get the picture. Should we worry about Natural Tunnel?

In the short term, in the span of a man's life, the Tunnel is as the Great Sphinx, silent, unchanging, inscrutable. But sometimes, when I've been down in the valley by myself, trying to piece together another part of the puzzle or straighten up the timeline, I swear I've heard it chuckle.

Certainly, man, with his machines and his whim, could make it disappear in an instant. He has changed it a little bit, snipped at it a little bit, filled it a little bit. But when the coal runs out in Southwest Virginia—and it will—and the railroad no longer runs, Stock Creek, on one warm spring day, will simply flush it all away.

When the glaciers come back—and they will—the yew will flourish and witness the clogging of the North Portal by rocks and trees washed down from the highlands. Maybe enough debris will clog the entrance, and the northern valley of Stock Creek will flood to form a lake, spilling over Tunnel Gap.

Every year Natural Tunnel gets just a little bit lower, a little bit shorter. It is most assuredly wearing away, and in a million years or so, it will have dissolved and flushed away to the Gulf of Mexico. There the calcium ions will be taken up, once again, by the little critters living there, recycled into shell and bone and then turned over again to become limy sediment, then limestone and dolostone.

Plate tectonics will gather these rocks into its conveyor belt, crash them into some continent, and leave them there to begin the erosion cycle all over again. Perhaps in that distant future there will be another, even greater Natural Tunnel.

But that's a long time off. None of us will see it, and one wonders if any man will.

Not to worry. The stones endure.

APPENDIX A: NATURAL TUNNEL AT A GLANCE

What is Natural Tunnel?	Natural Tunnel is one of the greatest examples of a particular type of karst formation in the world. In geologic terminology, a natural tunnel is defined as "a cave that is nearly horizontal and that is open at both ends. It may contain a stream. Synonyms include tunnel and tunnel cave." Natural Tunnel is notable in that, besides a stream, a working railroad passes through it, and a road passes over it. The northern and southern approaches to the Tunnel are notable for their sheer cliffs, called amphitheaters; the southern is the most spectacular. Natural Tunnel was operated as a tourist attraction from 1928 to 1967 before becoming a state park.
Where is Natural Tunnel?	Natural Tunnel is in western Scott County, Virginia. The nearest town is Duffield. Natural Tunnel is located approximately one mile off U.S. Route 23/58/421 near the junction of routes 871 and 646. Natural Tunnel is found on the USGS 7½-minute Clinchport Quadrangle at the following coordinates:

Location	Universal Transverse Mercator 17	Latitude / Longitude
Route 646 directly over the Tunnel	344235E 4063258N	36° 42' 15" N 82° 44' 38" W
South Portal where tracks enter the Tunnel	344194E 4063075N	36° 42' 09" N 82° 44' 39" W
North Portal where tracks enter the Tunnel	344250E 4063324N	36° 42' 17" N 82° 44' 37" W

What rocks did Natural Tunnel form in?	Natural Tunnel formed in strata, predominantly dolostone, of the Knox Group of Cambro-Ordovician age, deposited approximately 500 million years ago.

Why did Natural Tunnel form at its particular location?	Dissolution was preferentially located along the Glenita Fault, which formed approximately 250 million years ago during the Appalachian Orogeny.
How long did it take Natural Tunnel to form?	The exact time is uncertain, but it likely occurred over the past 750,000 to 1,000,000 years. Natural Tunnel has probably been in its present form for the past 10,000 years.
How long is Natural Tunnel?	The length of Natural Tunnel is dependent on the points measured. In a straight line from the overhang at the South Portal to the vertical face at the North Portal, the distance is 763 feet. Following the curve of the railroad track from these same points, the distance is 838 feet. If one follows the Stock Creek stream channel, the distance is over 900 feet.
How wide is Natural Tunnel?	For most of its length, Natural Tunnel is approximately 100 feet wide. It is up to 200 feet across at its widest point.
How high is the roof inside the Tunnel?	The height of the roof varies throughout the Tunnel but averages approximately 50 feet. The highest points are 70-80 feet.
How high are the amphitheaters?	The height of the sheer walls of the North and South Portal is dependent on the upper point measured. The following lists the heights of points above Stock Creek: South Portal to the Eagle's Nest—280 feet; to edge of vegetation—350 feet; to Lover's Leap and the Tower—400 feet; to nearest high point of Purchase Ridge (park campground)—550 feet. North Portal to Route 646—250 feet.
How far is it across the Amphitheater?	It is approximately 400 feet from the Eagle's Nest to Lover's Leap. Traveling on foot, it is nearly a quarter mile from the Eagle's Nest to Lover's Leap.
Who owns Natural Tunnel?	Natural Tunnel, the centerpiece of Natural Tunnel State Park, is the property of the Commonwealth of Virginia. Norfolk Southern Railway Corporation has a right-of-way for its track through the Tunnel and along Stock Creek.

APPENDIX B: NATURAL TUNNEL DIARIES

The following diary entries, except for the last one, are purely fictional, simply flights of fancy by the author, and should not be misconstrued as real. They take facts and happenings in the story of Natural Tunnel and place them in the words of fictional characters, though certainly the latter are based, in part, on real people. The results are vignettes I hope will assist the reader in understanding how past visitors might have experienced the Tunnel.

[Editor's note: The following diary entries use the spelling and punctuation of their respective "original" authors.]

April 13, 1783: 3 days hard walk from the Blockhouse, crossed Clinch just above Troublesome Creek. Water up to waist, sent Jason across with grapevines, lashed double at joints. Men had little problem, but ladies had to move as pack, some with babes in arms. Poor little Madeline, footsore but never cried, rode across on Jason's back, all the way to camp in tight valley before next ridge. Followed game trail through cliffs this eventide, shot doe at small flat, shot like thunder under magnificent cliffs around big cave full of rock and tree wash. On return to camp with haunches, Peterson said he'd seen Indian sign northwest of camp. We must push to Little Flat Lick tomorrow, try to catch Herron's party.

November 6, 1821: Jacob returned from his trapline last night with but two poor beaver, and telling the tale of the branch disappearing into a great maw. Determined to see, Rothchild and I left the foot of Powell and traveled about 3 miles south, skirting beaver ponds which made for hard go in part. Flushed bear and two cubs in cane thicket, gave the horses quite a start, throwing William into a great hollow sycamore, but no real damage. Jacob, while exaggerative in his stories for the most part, did this one little justice. Came upon great keyhole (100 feet high?), the branch throwing itself at a great wall of stone before sweeping to the west. Peculiar smell in rocks at upper left of entrance, found catamount prints, which caused us to halfcock for the rest of the exploration. With pine faggot followed creek around wall into great room with boulders as big as Regis Tavern, and to a great debouchement and palisade hollow. Sign of much digging here, but for reasons I have yet to fathom, much less by whom. Seem to recall a paper read by a young man of Jefferson's about such a place, will try to dig it out when I return to Philadelphia.

June 18, 1842: If there's one word that could describe such a horrid place, it must be "filthy"! Even though late yesterday, and with many miles to go, I shook my finger in Peter's face and said "Onward, and now!" He knows my moods, and not too keen on the prospects of a tavern bed in a shared room, we hired a young boy, barefoot and grinning, to lead the way. 10 miles out of Estillville I nodded off in the saddle with a firm grip, but came fully awake when my horse made the plunge into the Clinch. Wet to the knees and sore to the soul, after another hour's ride our arrival at Dotson's cabin was loudly announced by a rush of flop-eared hounds shying the horses and bounding about the clearing, soon quieted by bearded Dotson's cursing, standing there in his greatshirt, oil lantern in one hand and long rifle in the other. Peter and I were led to a lean-to shed on the cabin's wall where I fell quickly and utterly asleep on a mat of hay.

This morning I awoke to a breeze wafting the delicious aroma of Mrs. Dotson's corncakes and fatback and was then led by shy—and obviously beautiful under the ashes on her cheek—Melinda to the "ladies' place." Upon completion of my toilet, Peter and I had that simple but filling breakfast—washed down with a tea made from the bark of some tree, but delightfully sweetened with honey—at a great plank table with a boisterous and excited brood of younglings that I never quite got the count of with their coming and going. Mrs. Dotson fills a basket with her corncakes and smoked meats for our walk—Gilmer, our young guide who it turns out is the nephew of Mr. Dotson, assures me it is only less than a mile to the great Sink of the Stock—while I try to catch this poor diary up. I do so hope this lark is better than the so-called "vistas" I have seen since we left Charleston, though I must admit the view from the Blue Ridge was breathtaking. But what could be the draw of this hole in the ground? Well, enough, perhaps I can say tomorrow here should Peter and I survive the trip, much less this flock of Dotson siblings fluttering outside the door!

May 4, 1851: The locals call it "Purchase," but I'll be damned if I'd buy the damned ridge. Too up and down, no way we could cut and grade over it. Mr. Garnett wants a route, and by gum he'll get one, but I don't know how we'll get over this one. Moccasin Gap is the sure way through the Clinch, but since then it'll be bridge after bridge and cut after cut. Old man name of Horton wandered into the camp last night, scared the hell out of young Seaver when he just appeared there by the fire, holding that old flintlock and his flophat low on his eyes. Seaver nearly broke the survey rod in his haste to get to his gun. The boy's too jumpy, don't know the ways of these mountain men, but that's an Ohio city boy for you. He asked for whiskey, but he took coffee, found out why we're here and said we ought to follow Stock, something about a "natural" tunnel in Purchase. Sounds like Horton wants to get a laugh at our expense, but that's the way we're going anyway. We'll see.

July 1, 1863: Per the Colonel's orders, today we moved the vats to the north entrance of the Stock Creek Sink, and below a spring flowing in a small hollow to Stock from the west, which should serve as a good source of water and preclude the work of toting by buckets up from the creek. Following muster I sent Privates Cawood and Stewart up the ridge above the spring to investigate the cave Farmer Bowlin told me of last night, but do not expect them back before evening mess. Given the setting of this Sink, I expected little if any chance of finding peter dirt in it, but young John-Jack reported in at noon of a small ledge in the large room about midway in the sink, a bag of promising earth in one hand, and an old hoe he'd found tucked in the back of the ledge in the other. I directed him and his cousin Gilmer to start digging and bringing to this place. Were it not for the help of these locals, our task would be an impossible one. I directed Sargents Richardson and Dillon to traverse the ridge to our north, called Cove, for likely signs of openings.

The Colonel in his last correspondence indicated scouts had seen no sign of Union activity in the area, but I am wary what with the many eyes of the natives of unknown allegiance in the neighborhood. A patrol of irregulars through yesterday had no news of the Southern Theatre, but spoke of mass movement in the Northern Virginia Theatre. It would be my surmise that General Lee has again moved the Army east towards Washington, there being little advantage to move west and even less to take the troops north into the enemy's homeland.

July 17, 1880: Were it not for the quick movement of Mr. Speer today, I fear that my livelihood would have been dealt a serious, if not crushing, blow. A sudden surge in the current bucked the raft, sliding my camera out the back of the wagon, but letting go of the towline he managed to grab it before tipping out. Thank goodness I had the presence of mind to encase the plates in Jean's old quilt.

The ride to the Tunnel was uneventful, as was the rest of my day, though busy in the extreme as I seemed to be continually breaking down and setting up, with many a long walk, if not climb, in between. Isaac was kind enough to help me when he could though James called him over often to speak with some local men and women who seemed to have come that day expressly to talk to him. On the way back to the Speers place I inquired of James what it was all about, but he seemed reluctant to speak of their meeting, saying only, "Glory, old son, glory." Enigmatic, to say the least. But I trust the photographs will sell well.

August 21, 1904: Rosa and me caught V&SW at Oreton at 9:00, got Tunnel at 9:45, late cause cow on tracks at Horton's Summit. Good band playing and much dancing, and lots of eats by the Walkers. Rumor was some jugs of Cope's 'shine was cached in woods other side of Little Tunnel, many boys made the walk that way, but slow coming back. Marty and Robert came back to Pavilion arguing, got into fist fight, broke banjo when Marty took a hard one, and Robert pert near knocked Rosa over railing. Captin Grubb cracked both in head with oil can, took money for banjo off Marty, threw both in coal tender. Trouble making grade to Horton's due to little sand, got Rosa home 3:00, her momma waiting at door. No kiss.

October 30, 1929: Stopped by the Kinel place today. Saundra loves that high rock they call the Eagle's Nest, but Nancy and I can't stand to get near the edge. When we pulled in we saw they had company and were fixing to back out when James came out on the porch and waved us in. We went in and met a Mr. Seaton, who was visiting, then Saundra went on up to that rock. We had a cup of coffee and left.

That Mr. Seaton was talking to James about selling the old place, which I find funny. Why anybody would want that rocky ground not worth farming, and so near to that drop off, I'll never know. Maybe he wants to use it for a hunting cabin.

The radio is all a buzz about some kind of crash

in New York yesterday, but I couldn't understand it. Maybe Ginger can explain it to me when she gets back.

July 3, 1941: I was dumbstruck today! There I am, painting on the fence next to the gift shop, up pulls a big sedan, and out steps Eleanor Roosevelt! The wife of the President of the United States! Next thing I know, I'm following her around, as is everybody else on the property. She was very nice, but she didn't stay long, only walked up to the overlook and looked down at the Tunnel. Said it was a "wonder." Just after she left, Rosalee called over to the paper in Gate City, told him she was heading that way. I can't wait to see what they write up about her!

And more exciting news today! Got a letter from Kyle, only second one since he went off to the Navy. He says he's going to be posted to Pearl, and he's bucking for a berth on the Arizona!

June 26, 1962: Sometimes I wonder why we ever left Michigan in this '56 Ford wagon. Ohio was okay because it's so flat, but once we hit eastern Kentucky, the kids started complaining. Jodie got sick near Pikeville and we had to pull over. Jill got sick in Jenkins and we had to pull over. Then we're just out of Duffield and Bob gets sick, and then both girls got sick again. I told Kenny we'd had enough so we've stopped for the night at a place called Natural Tunnel.

The manager took one look at the kids and the back of the wagon, and suggested we use their little campground for the night. I finally got the car cleaned up, a little food down the kids, and them in their sleeping bags, and I feel like I could cry. Kenny wants to take the kids down to see that Tun-

nel in the morning, but I just don't know. Right now all I want to do is sleep.

June 16, 1967: I can't believe this old Ford is still running, but Kenny has babied it over the years. It got us here just fine, but these Kentucky and Virginia roads haven't improved much. At least the kids are older, and while they may get queasy, they can hold it.

But, oh, what a shock when we stopped at the Tunnel and found it's not open now! We had had so much fun here when we stopped, when, 5 years ago? It's been sold to the state of Virginia, they're going to make a state park out of it. That nice man who was fixing up the old lodge said you couldn't stay overnight anymore. Kenny told him about the last time we stopped, and he just laughed. He said he had to go home then, but as he was leaving, he waved Kenny over to his truck. When Kenny came back he said that nice man told him he was going to lock the gate on the way out and he would let us out in the morning, but if anybody found us here, he didn't know anything about it!

So, I've just made the last of the bologna sandwiches, but we've got lots of cheese, and lots of bread, and lots of pop. The kids took off down the trails and Kenny's got a little fire going in an old camping grate. We'll roast marshmallows later. We've got the whole place to ourselves, who would have ever thought it? I wonder if we can come back when they turn it into a park?

August 31, 1987: Had the family reunion at the Tunnel today. Heard they were having a walk-through of the Tunnel, took the grandkids. Some geologist led the trip, talking about water and faults having made the Tunnel, but I never quite got it. Mighty cool inside and plain exciting when a coal train came rolling through. Walking up the hill Jimmy found a rock, showed it to the geologist, who told him it was a fossil "something-lite" but that you couldn't remove them from state parks. Jimmy put it back where he picked it up, but he sniffed a little bit.

We were getting ready to leave when that geologist came over to the car and told Jimmy, son-of-a-gun, he just happened to have a "something-lite" in his pack and would he like to have it. Jimmy grinned and almost jumped out of his seat belt. I took a look at it, and it was the same one Jimmy had picked up.

December 1, 2002: Second rejection letter came in today. Seeing that I only mailed the manuscripts out less than a month ago, I guess they're prompt, if nothing else. Is anybody interested in this story? I love the place, as do thousands, if not millions, of others. And it's a story that needs telling. Whatever. Stay focused. Plan on going to the Scott County Library and see if I can dig any more gems out of the microfilmed newspapers. . . .

APPENDIX C: IMPORTANT EVENTS IN THE HISTORY OF NATURAL TUNNEL

500 Million Years Ago	The rocks Natural Tunnel will form in are deposited in a shallow, warm sea. These rocks, predominantly dolostone, will come to be called the Knox Group.
250 Million Years Ago	Eastern North America collides with western North Africa in the Appalachian Orogeny, the great mountain-building episode, folding and faulting the Knox Group (and underlying and overlying rocks). The Rye Cove Syncline and, most importantly, the Glenita Fault are formed. In ensuing time, the great thickness of rocks above the present-day landscape is eroded and worn down, ultimately exposing the Glenita Fault to waters near the surface.
1,000,000 Years Ago	Dissolution of the dolostone, concurrent with erosional lowering of the earth's surface, forms Natural Tunnel.
12,000 Years Ago	The first eastern North American hunter-gatherers, following game and/or foraging, are likely the first humans to see Natural Tunnel.
Pre-Colonial America	Natural Tunnel lies within the domain of the Cherokee Nation, adjacent to the Shawnee hunting lands, and is probably visited by both tribes. Daniel Boone and party, blazing the Wilderness Road to Kentucky in 1775, likely become the first people of European descent to see Natural Tunnel. It is possible Boone may have seen the area even sooner, having passed through as early as 1769.
1814	Mathew Carey's map of Virginia denotes "Natural Bridge" in the location of Natural Tunnel.
1818	Francis Walker Gilmer reads his paper "On the Geological Formation of the Natural Bridge of Virginia" before the American Philosophical Society, comparing the formation of Natural Bridge (and refuting Thomas Jefferson's theory of upheaval) to "over Stock Creek, a branch of Clinch River, a bridge. . . ."
1822	Map by H. C. Carey and I. Lea denotes "Natural Bridge" in the location of Natural Tunnel.

1831	Lieutenant Colonel Stephen H. Long visits Natural Tunnel on orders of the U. S. Topographical Bureau, as part of a study of a wagon route from Linville, North Carolina, to Pikeville, Kentucky. His report to the commissioners at the Estillville Convention makes no mention of Natural Tunnel, obviously not a choice passage for a wagon route.
1832	Long publishes "Description of a Natural Tunnel in Scott County, Virginia" in the *Monthly American Journal of Geology*. He is the first to use the term "tunnel" and can be credited with naming the feature. He is also the first to publish a wood engraving (artist unknown) of the Tunnel, showing a view of the South Portal. *The Mirror of Literature, Amusement and Instruction* of London, England, publishes an abridged version of Long's article and an embellished version of his wood engraving.
1838	Thomas G. Bradford's map shows "Natural Tunnel."
Note: From this time on, Natural Tunnel, sometimes referred to as "Natural Bridge" even after the naming by Long, appears regularly on historical maps. It is apparently firmly ensconced on the American landscape; further listings of separate maps will not be included here.	
1839	The Reverend H. Ruffner, rector of Washington College (later to become Washington and Lee University), in his "Notes of a Tour from Virginia to Tennessee, in the Months of July and August, 1838," published in the *Southern Literary Messenger* in April, writes of a conversation with a "gentleman of Tennessee." Ruffner still calls it a "natural bridge" but points out that it is more rightly called a tunnel. Ruffner compares and contrasts Natural Tunnel with Natural Bridge; he is apparently unaware of the work of Gilmer and Long. In July, Ruffner publishes in the same magazine "Judith Bensaddi: A Tale," and with a more literary bent in a fanciful story, relates the same as above.
1844	In a letter to the editor of the *Southern Literary Messenger,* a writer (could this be Reverend Ruffner's friend?) known only by the initials, "W. H. C." describes a visit to the Tunnel. He notes the previous lack of visitors to the place due to its remote location, but indicates the situation will change due to a "capital road lately constructed." Importantly, he notes the evidence of saltpeter workings. Further, we are first introduced to the story of Poor Dotson, swinging on an unraveling rope from the cliff above the Tunnel.
1845	Henry Howe publishes *Historical Collections of Virginia*. The entry on Scott County is almost entirely devoted to a description of the Tunnel, quoting much of Long's paper, and a telling of the Dotson story. Engravings of a view looking out the South Portal, and of Dotson hanging from his rope, accompany the Scott County section.

1848	The Virginia & Tennessee Railroad is organized.
1850	The article "Summer Travel in the South," in the *Southern Quarterly Review,* contains a passing reference to the Tunnel.
1851	Henry Howe's *Historical Collections of the Great West* contains a chapter entitled "The Natural Tunnel." Howe repeats Long's description almost word for word, though not giving credit as per his 1845 *Historical Collections of Virginia.* The story of Dotson appears again. A wood engraving of a view looking out the South Portal accompanies the chapter, but it is not the same one as his 1845 book.
	Plagiarism again shows in *Debow's Review* in March, with the exact wording of the 1850 travelogue "Summer Travel in the South."
	Again, in "The Land of the Cherokee" in the *United States Democratic Review* in April, we read a travelogue of the south, with but a passing reference to the Tunnel. It would appear the Tunnel is always worthy of mention in such writings, but it is likely that the "capital road" described by W. H. C. in 1844 did not always suit these wayward travelers.
1852	An assistant to C. F. M. Garnett, chief engineer of the Virginia & Tennessee Railroad, conducts a reconnaissance survey of the Abingdon to Cumberland Gap route, preparing maps that show the Natural Tunnel as part of the planned route. (There is some indication this survey may have been conducted as early as 1849.)
	Hugh Murray's *The Encyclopaedia of Geography* gives a brief description of the Tunnel.
	The Virginia General Assembly authorizes the V&T to build a branch line to the Cumberland Gap. The V&T is unable, or unwilling, to complete the project.
1853	Richard Fisher's *A New and Complete Statistical Gazetteer of the United States of America,* referencing Stock Creek, notes the passage of the creek through the Tunnel. In future gazetteers such a reference is obligatory.
	C. F. M. Garnett, chief engineer of the V&T, files a report dated October 31, 1853, to the directors of the railroad on the proposed branch line from Abingdon to the Cumberland Gap. Describing the scenery, he notes, "The natural tunnel in Scott County and the large and beautiful cave in the same neighborhood are considerations which would alone attract crowds of visitors. . . ."
	A new company, the Virginia and Kentucky Railroad, is formed by interested Southwest Virginians, succeeding to the rights of the V&T. Little was done on the railroad route from Abingdon to the Cumberland Gap, and the Civil War halted all work.

1855	The Reverend C. Collins, president of Emory and Henry College and professor of moral and mental science, writes an article in the October issue of the *Ladies' Repository,* titled "Virginia's Two Bridges," continuing the theme of comparison between Natural Bridge and Natural Tunnel. His description of the Tunnel, though in florid language, is suspiciously reminiscent of Howe's, who borrowed freely from Long. Further, Collins references Howe's Dotson story, taking the liberty to "correct his figures." Richard Edwards's *Statistical Gazetteer of the State of Virginia* contains the obligatory description of the Tunnel, as does J. Calvin Smith's *Harper's Statistical Gazetteer of the World.*
1856	Charles Lanman, a journalist and artist, describes the Tunnel in his *Adventures in the Wilds of the United States and British American Provinces.* His description, so much like others before, does not read like a firsthand account. Lippincott's *Pronouncing Gazetteer* contains a description of the Tunnel in the exact wording of Richard Edwards's gazetteer of the previous year.
1857	*Harper's New Monthly Magazine* publishes "Winter in the South," a fanciful dialogue of a family's trip to the Southwest Virginia/Upper East Tennessee area. The description of the Tunnel and its environs appears to be a firsthand account. Importantly, wood engravings supply views of the area, and the description (and engraving) of the Tunnel interior implies structures no longer visible today due to railroad construction. The book *Adventures of Hunters and Travellers, and Narratives of Border Warfare,* by an author noted only as "An Old Hunter," is published. A short chapter retells the Dotson story and curiously describes the roof of the Tunnel as 900 feet high while stating that the Amphitheater walls are 300 feet high. An engraving, probably the most outrageous, implies that it is possible to see completely through the Tunnel.
1859	*The New American Cyclopaedia* gives a quick reference under a Scott County heading. William Beverhout Thompson, chief engineer of the Virginia & Kentucky Railroad, reports to the company's board of directors about a resurvey "following generally the route formerly surveyed by Col. Garnette" of the proposed line from Abingdon to the Cumberland Gap, noting the benefit of using the Tunnel.
1860	*Illustrations of Surface Geology* by Edward Hitchcock, former president of Amherst College and state geologist of Vermont, does not contain a description of the Tunnel but rather the valley it lies in; Mr. Hitchcock seems more concerned with surface topography due to erosion. His brief description appears to be a secondhand account.

1861	Noted illustrator and historian John Warner Barber joins with Henry Howe to publish *Our Whole Country: Or the Past and Present of the United States, Historical and Descriptive*. Interestingly, the description of the Tunnel is brief, and no illustration is included.
1863	Saltpeter is mined in Natural Tunnel and nearby caves by members of the 25th Virginia Regiment for the Confederate war effort.
1866	*Appletons' Hand-Book of American Travel* by Edward Hall is another guide for the traveler with a passing reference to the Tunnel. In Estillville, R. W. Hughes, Esq., president of the V&K, delivers a speech to fellow officers, directors, and stockholders of the company. He urges them to take hold of the project again, now that the Civil War is over, and speaks glowingly of coal, and particularly iron-ore reserves, along the route of the railroad. Regarding the route, he states, "The Natural tunnel and Creek Valley present themselves for the transit through Purchase Ridge."
1869	The V&T consolidates with the Norfolk and Petersburg, the Southside, and the V&K to form the Atlantic, Mississippi and Ohio Railroad. A stipulation of consolidation was that the AM&O had to build the branch line to the Cumberland Gap, if the railroad in Kentucky built its line to the same. Kentucky never followed through, which relieved the AM&O of its obligation.
1870	W. S. Clark's *Illustrated History* . . . again, another passing reference. The *Hamilton Literary Magazine* contains an article (author known only by the initials "R. L. B.") entitled "The Natural Bridge." In florid prose, the author describes the Tunnel and again recounts the story of Poor Dodson/Dotson. Importantly, though, the author references a survey for a railroad done "about ten years ago" and indicates that one will pass through the Tunnel in "a few years more."
1871	*The Virginia Tourist* by Edward A. Pollard contains an excellent (if, again, florid) description of the Tunnel (with engravings by Van Ingen and Snyder) and the difficulty in traveling there. Here we first see the tragic tale of the death of Indian lovers by falls from Lover's Leap (a murder followed by suicide), and again we read the story of Poor Dodson/Dotson. Importantly, we also read a description of "The Cave of the Unknown," located half a mile from the Tunnel; it is Bowlin Cave. James Dabney McCabe's *The Great Republic* contains an engraving of the Tunnel, the same engraving used in Pollard's book, though it is labeled "Natural Bridge," and the accompanying narrative describes that feature. Obviously, Mr. McCabe had never seen the Tunnel, nor does he mention it in his book.

1872	*Chamber's Encyclopaedia* contains a passing reference to the Tunnel. The *Richmond Daily Whig*, in the September 14 edition, publishes correspondence from an unknown writer, entitled "The Tunnel and Cave in Scott County." Even if the writer does refer to the rocks as "granite," the report appears firsthand, describing the large boulders, logs, and driftwood in the Tunnel, and including a description of a visit to Bowlin Cave.
1873	The *American Cyclopaedia* contains a passing reference to the Tunnel.
1874	*Scribner's Monthly* contains "The Great South: A Ramble in Virginia," an article in a series by Edward King that gives a brief description of the Tunnel and passing reference to a nearby "massive cave" (Bowlin). Importantly, it states, "In a few years, it is confidently expected, a railroad will find its way through this wonderful tunnel, and the locomotive's scream will be heard on the path over which Daniel Boone painfully toiled. . . ." *Picturesque America* is published under the auspices of William Cullen Bryant, considered by some the first American poet to win international acclaim. The description of the Tunnel (though whether by Bryant is uncertain) verges on the poetic, and there is the inevitable comparison with Natural Bridge. Included are two wood engravings by William L. Sheppard—an interior view that cannot be seen today, and a view looking out of the South Portal. Additionally, citing the difficulty in reaching the Tunnel, the narrative notes how the future traveler will fare better when the railroad is built, stating, "It is said that the projected road must pass through this tunnel, there being no other practicable route," though the writer laments the impact such construction might have on the beauty of the Tunnel.
1875	Edward King, apparently pleased with the reception of his articles, publishes them in book form; the portion describing the Tunnel is unchanged. Johnson's *New Universal Cyclopaedia* contains a passing reference to the Tunnel but incorrectly puts the Tunnel in Clinch Mountain, with the Clinch River flowing through it.
1876	The Bristol Coal and Iron Narrow Gauge Railway is formed, succeeding to the franchise and right-of-way of the defunct V&K. Financial troubles soon cause failure.
1878	Charles B. Coale publishes *The Life and Adventures of Wilburn Waters,* containing a chapter titled "The Natural Bridge of Scott." Mr. Coale's description sounds suspiciously like many done before. He repeats the story of poor Dodson/Dotson, but he calls him "Horton" and places him in his precarious position at the end of his rope hunting for *(cont.)*

1878 *(cont.)*	"Peter dirt" during the War of 1812. Coale states that "the track of the Virginia and Kentucky railroad is located [meaning a survey has been conducted] through [the Tunnel]," and that the "Natural Bridge" will become a popular attraction, "should that road ever be made."
1880	W. W. James, I. C. Fowler, and W. D. Jones purchase "seventy acres, more or less . . . embracing the Natural Bridge and Tunnel" from William P. and Emily Good, Martin and Eliza Hill, Jesse and Jane Bishop, and Charles and Esther Horton.
1881	John J. Stevenson, professor of geology at the University of the City of New York, presents a paper to the American Philosophical Society on January 21. He provides a brief description of the Tunnel and notes, "The surveyed line of the [NG] railroad passes through it." The editor's column of the *Bristol News* reports, "Messrs. [W. W.] James and [I. C.] Fowler [the editor] returned last week from the Natural Tunnel, where they laid off the coming town of Jamesville."
1882	By act of the Virginia General Assembly, the name of the Bristol Coal and Iron Narrow Gauge Railway is changed to the South Atlantic and Ohio. By act of the Virginia General Assembly, the Great Natural Bridge and Tunnel Company is incorporated, with I. C. Fowler, W. W. James, Sr., W. D. Jones, and Elbert Fowler as organizers. An article in the *Bristol News,* reprinted from the *Richmond Dispatch,* states, "A Mr. [W. D.] Jones of Philadelphia, Mr. [W. W.] James, and Mr. I. C. Fowler [editor of the *Bristol News*] have purchased the Natural Tunnel in Scott County, Virginia." Mr. and Mrs. W. W. James, Sr., and Mr. and Mrs. W. D. Jones convey to the SA&O the right to construct a railroad bed through the Tunnel. The deed stipulates that control of access to the Tunnel lies solely with James and Jones and that the SA&O will build a depot "on the tract of land conveyed by William P. Good," and a platform at the mouth of the Tunnel. Most notably, the deed further stipulates, "The said railroad company is further to remove all materials, such as dirt . . . not used in constructing their roadbed to a convenient distance from the mouth of said tunnel . . . to conduct their work . . . in a prudent and careful manner, so as not to mar or disfigure the natural appearance of said tunnel more than will occasionally result from building their road." James and Jones apparently recognized the economic opportunity railroad access would create and wanted the natural appearance preserved as much as possible.

1886	The September 3 issue of the *Philadelphia Evening Record* reports, "Mr. William D. Jones, of Philadelphia, who has been the proud owner of probably the only natural tunnel in this country, gave it away the other day to a railroad company [the SA&O]."
1887	*Caverns and Cavern Life,* by Nathaniel Southgate Shaler, professor of geology at Harvard University and former state geologist of Kentucky, describes natural tunnels in the eastern United States and rightly points out that the finest example is Natural Tunnel. Interestingly, he notes, "This natural way is about to be used for the passage of a railway."
1888-1890	The roadbed though the Tunnel is laid and two small tunnels constructed, one in the Tunnel near the North Portal, forming a man-made opening adjacent to the natural opening, and the other through the rib of dolostone that forms the south end of the Amphitheater.
1889	*July 1.* I. C. Fowler and wife convey their ⅓ interest in the Natural Tunnel property to the Virginia, Tennessee & Carolina Steel & Iron Company for $3,026. *October 1.* W. W. James and wife convey their Natural Tunnel property to the VT&CS&IC. The deed directs the payoff of W. D. Jones's ⅓ share for $4,000, with $8,000 to go to James.
1890	*May 15.* The first regularly scheduled passenger train from Bristol passes through the Tunnel en route to Big Stone Gap. *June 10.* The first train of coal passes through the Tunnel en route to Bristol.
1891	The SA&O uses the appellation "The Natural Tunnel Route."
1893	Emile Low, an engineer at the Mathieson Alkali Works in Saltville, Virginia, in a letter to the *Engineering News,* reports on his observations of the Tunnel and railroad construction after a visit in March. Mr. Low makes three interesting points: he confirms the original course of Stock Creek through the Tunnel; he observes that "some work" had been done on a different roadbed than now used, which involved cutting off some of the toe of the cliff forming the southern extremity of the Amphitheater (his term, the "rotunda"), that was abandoned for construction of the "Little Tunnel"; and he notes that Stock Creek, at low flow, sinks about ⅛ mile above the North Portal and reissues below the Tunnel at numerous points, including one outlet "in the bed of the stream, where it bubbles up like a miniature geyser."

1894	The U.S. Geological Survey publishes the "Estillville Folio, Kentucky-Virginia-Tennessee" by Marius R. Campbell. The included topographic map, dated "1882-3-8," shows the SA&O traversing Natural Tunnel. Interestingly, there is a settlement just north of Natural Tunnel named "Tunnel." In a discussion of stream drainages in the area, Campbell writes, "Through the limestone ridge north of Clinchport Stock Creek has cut an interesting tunnel, whose southern entrance is picturesque, consisting of a magnificent portal opening from a wild and rugged ravine. The tunnel is now utilized by the South Atlantic and Ohio Railroad, and is an important scenic feature of that route."
1899	*February 17.* The Virginia & Southwestern Railway Company, as the result of decree from Judge John Paul of the U.S. Court for the Western District of Virginia, purchases the SA&O. A few days later, the V&SW also takes possession of the Bristol, Elizabethton and North Carolina Railroad. *June 15.* The Interstate Coal & Iron Company purchases the Natural Tunnel property, as well as many other Southwest Virginia properties, from the Virginia, Tennessee & Carolina Steel & Iron Company.
1901	*December 14.* The *Denton* (Maryland) *Journal* reprints the article, from the *Scott County Leader,* "A Natural Tunnel, As Interesting a Curiosity as Virginia's Natural Bridge." *With the World's Greatest Travellers* includes Pollard's 1871 description of the Tunnel.
1902	The January 3 issue of the *Elizabethton Mountaineer* reports, "The managers of the traffic department of the Virginia & Southwestern Railway have been sending out a neatly printed and nicely covered holiday card of greeting. The card contains an excellent picture of the 'East Entrance to the Natural Tunnel' in Virginia."
1907	The Pavilion at the South Portal is in existence by this date, as evinced by old postcards, though likely constructed earlier.
1908	E. H. Walker purchases Natural Tunnel from the Interstate Coal & Iron Company (vendor's lien is satisfied November 8, 1909).
1910	The Southern Railway acquires a controlling interest in the V&SW, though the V&SW continues to operate semi-independently. The name "The Natural Tunnel Route" is dropped, and the railroad apparently no longer actively promotes the Tunnel as a tourist attraction.
1916	Southern Railway takes control of the V&SW and formally incorporates the trackage into their system.

1925	E. H. Walker and wife convey ¾ interest in the Natural Tunnel property to B. H. Quillen, E. D. Rollins, and W. H. Perry.
1928	The Natural Tunnel and Caverns Corporation incorporates. Equal owners are B. H. Quillen, E. D. Rollins, W. H. Perry, and E. H. Walker. The corporation allows access to the Tunnel via Glenita and the Little Tunnel on weekends, at 50 cents per person. The NT&CC enters a lease with Joseph P. Seaton, doing business as The Natural Tunnel Amusement Company, with the stipulation that Mr. Seaton invests $10,000 to develop the property.
1930	The Natural Tunnel and Caverns Corporation terminates the lease with Joseph Seaton due to non-expenditure of the agreed sum but pays Mr. Seaton for his purchase of the property that is the present entranceway to Natural Tunnel State Park.
1931	Natural Tunnel and Caverns Corporation formally opens as a tourist attraction. The opening, on August 25, is broadcast over the only local radio station, WOPI of Bristol, Virginia, and includes area musicians and a poem for the occasion written and read by Mrs. Julia A. Walker.
1936	Herbert P. Woodward, director of the Division of Natural Sciences at the University of Newark, publishes "Natural Bridge and Natural Tunnel, Virginia" in the *Journal of Geology*. Continuing the theme comparing the two Virginia wonders, Woodward cites similar geologic settings and the role of underground stream piracy and cavern collapse in the formation of both.
1937-1938	The NT&CC approaches both the Natural Bridge Corporation and the Colonial Williamsburg Foundation (created by the philanthropy of John D. Rockefeller, Jr.) in an attempt to sell the Natural Tunnel property. Both entities reject the purchase based on the distance from their operations and the remoteness of Natural Tunnel.
1939	E. H. Walker dies (his wife, Julia A., dies the next year), with the other owners subsequently buying out his interest in the NT&CC. On May 6, the passenger train "The Lonesome Pine Special" makes its last run through Natural Tunnel. The Natural Tunnel, Chasm and Caverns Corporation (NTC&CC) incorporates under the laws of the Commonwealth of Virginia on December 8. Officers are Edmonds D. Rollins, Belt H. Quillen, Rex R. Thompson, Samuel F. Freels, and Cecil D. Quillen. The company is authorized to issue capital stock up to $95,000, including 3,000 shares of preferred stock at $20 per share, and 350,000 shares of common stock at 10 cents per share.

1954	G. Alexander Robertson writes of his interview with "General" John Salling, the oldest surviving Virginia Civil War veteran (and one of only five alive at the time) in the *National Speleological Society News*. Mr. Salling tells of digging saltpeter—as Mr. Robertson eloquently states, "for the Confederacy at the time of the battle of Gettysburg"—in Natural Tunnel as a member of the 25th Virginia Regiment.
1955	Luther F. Addington provides a brief history of the Tunnel in the June issue of *Railway Progress,* attributing the "Eighth Wonder of the World" appellation to Theodore Roosevelt. Robert L. Scribner retells many of the legends associated with the Tunnel in the autumn issue of *Virginia Cavalcade.*
1963	The Virginia Division of Mineral Resources publishes *Report of Investigations 5,* "Geology of the Clinchport Quadrangle, Virginia" by William B. Brent. Brent notes the deformed rocks at the South Portal of Natural Tunnel but does not recognize them as evidence of faulting. William D. Thornbury, in his classic *Principles of Geomorphology,* references Woodward's theory for the formation of the Tunnel.
1964	H. H. Douglas, in his *Caves of Virginia,* includes a brief description of the Tunnel.
1967	Natural Tunnel is purchased by the Commonwealth of Virginia from the NTC&CC.
1971	Natural Tunnel State Park is opened for the public.
1975	The Virginia Division of Mineral Resources publishes *Descriptions of Virginia Caves,* by John R. Holsinger, containing a description of Natural Tunnel and the Shelter Caves.
1977	Natural Tunnel and the Shelter Caves are mapped by William C. Douty and others. The *National Railway Bulletin* publishes Gil Bledsoe's article "Early History of the Natural Tunnel Route."
1982	Southern Railway merges with Norfolk and Western, forming the Norfolk Southern Corporation.
1988	The British Cave Research Association publishes Tony Waltham's article "Natural Tunnel, Virginia" in *Cave Science*. Waltham disagrees with Woodward's theory of origin and assigns the Tunnel's formation to the capture of Stock Creek by a sinkhole at the present North Portal, entering a dissolution channel (the present Tunnel passage), and exiting as a spring at the present South Portal.

1990	The Virginia Division of Mineral Resources publishes "The Geology of Natural Tunnel State Park" by Robert C. Milici in *Virginia Minerals*. Milici rightly recognizes the fault present at the Tunnel location and names it Glenita Fault. It is important to note Milici was unaware of Waltham's work; his model of origin of the Tunnel is virtually identical to Waltham's; the only real difference is the recognition of the essential role of the fault.
1993	The Virginia Section of the American Institute of Professional Geologists maps Natural Tunnel Caverns.
1996	The Virginia Speleological Society maps Bolling (Bowlin) Cave.

Ownership of Natural Tunnel	
Pre-1880	Natural Tunnel is claimed to lie within the boundaries of four different owners: William P. and Emily Good, Martin and Eliza Hill, Jesse and Jane Bishop, and Charles and Esther Horton.
1880	William W. James, I. C. Fowler, and W. D. Jones purchase Natural Tunnel (and adjoining land) from the above, creating a distinct parcel.
1889	James, Fowler, and Jones sell Natural Tunnel to the Virginia, Tennessee & Carolina Steel & Iron Company.
1899	The Interstate Coal & Iron Company, by purchasing lands owned by the Virginia, Tennessee & Carolina Steel & Iron Company, gains the Tunnel property.
1908	Elbert H. Walker purchases Natural Tunnel from the Interstate Coal & Iron Company.
1925	E. H. Walker (and wife) sell ¾ interest in Natural Tunnel to Edmonds D. Rollins, W. H. Perry, and Belt H. Quillen.
1928	The Natural Tunnel and Caverns Corporation incorporates, with the four owners deeding their ownership to the corporation.
1939	The Natural Tunnel, Chasm and Caverns Corporation is formed, succeeding to ownership of Natural Tunnel.
1967	The Commonwealth of Virginia purchases Natural Tunnel from the Natural Tunnel, Chasm and Caverns Corporation.

Railroads and Natural Tunnel	
1888-1890	The South Atlantic and Ohio Railroad lays track through Natural Tunnel and begins coal, passenger, and freight operations.
1899	The Virginia & Southwestern Railway succeeds to the South Atlantic and Ohio Railroad's rights and trackage.
1906	The Southern Railway purchases controlling interest in the Virginia & Southwestern Railroad, but the latter continues to operate semi-autonomously under its own name.
1916	The Southern Railway formally incorporates the Virginia & Southwestern Railroad into the Southern system.
1939	Passenger service through Natural Tunnel ends.
1982	Southern Railway merges with Norfolk and Western to form the Norfolk Southern Railway.

BIBLIOGRAPHY

Addington, L. F. "Virginia's Natural Tunnel." *Railway Progress* 9, no. 4 (1955).

Addington, Robert M. *History of Scott County, Virginia*. 3rd ed. Johnson City, Tenn.: The Overmountain Press, 1992.

"Art. VI—The Bristol Convention." in *Debow's Review, Agricultural, Commercial, Industrial Progress and Resources* 5, no. 9 (1868).

Bachman, R. L. "The Natural Bridge." *Hamilton Literary Magazine,* January 1870: 176-179.

Barnard, Frederick A. P. and Arnold Guyot, eds. *Johnson's New Universal Cyclopaedia*. New York: A. J. Johnson and Son, 1875.

Bingham, Edgar. "Physiographic diagram of Virginia." *Virginia Division of Mineral Resources Publication* 105 (1991).

Bledsoe, S. G. "Early History of the Natural Tunnel Route." *National Railway Bulletin* 42, no. 2 (1977).

Brent, William B. "Geology of the Clinchport Quadrangle, Virginia." *Virginia Division of Mineral Resources Report of Investigations* 5 (1963).

Bryant, William Cullen, ed. *Picturesque America; Or the Land We Live In*. New York: D. Appleton and Company, 1872.

Campbell, Marius R. "Estillville Folio, Kentucky-Virginia-Tennessee." *Geologic Atlas U.S., Folio 12.* United States Geological Survey, Washington, D.C.: Government Printing Office, 1894.

Carey, M. "A Correct Map of Virginia." *Carey's General Atlas, Improved and Enlarged; Being a Collection of Maps of the World and Quarters, Their Principal Empires, Kingdoms, &c.* Philadelphia: by the author, 1814.

Carter, Russ., et al. "Bolling Cave Map." Virginia Speleological Survey: unpublished, 1996.

Chambers, W. and R. Chambers. *Chambers's Encyclopaedia*. Philadelphia: J. B. Lippincott and Company, 1872.

Clark, W. S. *Illustrated History, Comprising in a Condensed Form a History of the United States, a Geography of the Western Continent, and the Chief Objects of Interest on the Eastern Continent, Including a Historical and Descriptive Sketch of the Holy Land.* Rockford, Ill.: J. H. Clark & Co., 1870.

Coale, Charles B. *The Life and Adventures of Wilburn Waters*. Johnson City, Tenn.: The Overmountain Press, 1994.

Collins, Rev. C. "Virginia's Two Bridges." *The Ladies' Repository: A Monthly Periodical, Devoted to Literature, Arts and Religion* 15, no. 10 (1855).

Collings, Dave. "Bolling Cave, Scott County." *Speleo Digest*, April 1997.

Cooper, Byron N. "Industrial Limestones and Dolomites in Virginia." *Clinch Valley District, Virginia Division of Mineral Resources Bulletin* 66 (1945).

Davis, Richard Victor. "Vascular Flora of Natural Tunnel State Park, Scott County, Virginia." Master of science thesis, East Tennessee Sate University, 1979.

Douglas, H. H. *Caves of Virginia.* Falls Church, Va.: Virginia Cave Survey, 1964.

Douty, William C., et al. "Natural Tunnel Map." Unpublished, 1977.

Draper, Lyman C. *The Life of Daniel Boone.* Ted Franklin Belue, ed. Mechanicsburg, Pa.: Stackpole Books, 1998.

Eby, J. Brian. "The Geology and Mineral Resources of Wise County and the Coal-bearing Portion of Scott County, Virginia." *Virginia Geological Survey Bulletin* 24 (1923).

Edwards, Richard. *Statistical Gazetteer of the State of Virginia, Embracing Important Topographical and Historical Information From Recent and Original Sources, Together With the Results of the Last Census Population, in Most Cases, to 1854.* Richmond, Va.: by the author, 1855.

Fisher, Richard Swainson. *A New and Complete Statistical Gazetteer of the United States of America, Founded on and Compiled From Official Federal and State Returns, and the Seventh National Census.* New York: J. H. Colton, 1853.

Fleenor, Lawrence J. Jr. *The Bear Grass, a History.* Big Stone Gap, Va.: by the author, 1991.

Fugate, Clara Talton. *The Legend of Natural Tunnel.* Radford, Va.: Pocahontas Press, 1986.

Gary, Margaret, Robert McAfee, and Carol L. Wolfe, eds. *Glossary of Geology.* Washington: American Geological Institute, 1977.

Gilmer, Francis Walker. "On the Geological Formation of the Natural Bridge of Virginia." *Transactions of the American Philosophical Society* 1 (1818): 187-192

Gooch, Edwin O., Robert S. Wood, and William T. Parrott. "Sources of Aggregate Used in Virginia Highway Construction." *Virginia Division of Mineral Resources Mineral Resources Report* 1 (1960).

Hall, Edward H. *Appleton's Hand-Book of American Travel.* New York: D. Appleton and Company, 1866.

Harvey, Robert L. "Excerpt of a Speech on Railroad Heroes." Address delivered to the Kingsport Junior Book Club, 1994.

Hitchcock, Edward. *Illustrations of Surface Geology.* New York: D. Appleton and Company, 1860.

Holsinger, John R. "Natural Tunnel." *Virginia Cave Survey Report Form.* National Speleological Society, 1971.

_____. "Descriptions of Virginia Caves." *Virginia Division of Mineral Resources Bulletin* 85 (1975).

Holsinger, John R. and James A. Estes. "Natural Tunnel Caverns Map." Unpublished, 1976.

Howe, Henry. *Historical Collections of Virginia.* Charleston, S.C.: Babcock & Co., 1845.

_____. *Historical Collections of the Great West.* Cincinnati, Ohio: Howe and E. Morgan and Company, 1851.

Howe, Henry and John Warner Barber. *Our Whole Country.* Cincinnati, Ohio: by the authors, 1861.

Hughes, Robert William. "Art. VII.—Virginia—Her Internal Improvements and Development." *Debow's Review, Agricultural, Commercial, Industrial Progress and Resources* 3, no. 3 (1867).

Kincaid, Robert L. *The Wilderness Road.* Kingsport, Tenn.: Arcata Graphics, 1992.

King, Edward. "The Great South: A Ramble in Virginia." *Scribner's Monthly, an Illustrated Magazine for the People,* April 1874.

_____. *The Great South: A Record of Journeys in Louisiana, Texas, the Indian Territory, Missouri, Arkansas, Mississippi, Alabama, Georgia, Florida, South Carolina, North Carolina, Kentucky, Tennessee, Virginia, West Virginia, and Maryland.* Hartford, Conn.: American Publishing Company, 1875.

"The Land of the Cherokee." *The United States Democratic Review* 28, no. 154 (1851).

Lanman, Charles. *Adventures in the Wilds of the United States and British American Provinces.* Philadelphia: J. W. Moore, 1856.

Long, Stephen H. "Description of a Natural Tunnel, in Scott County, Virginia." *Monthly American Journal of Geology and Natural Science* 1, no. 8 (1832): 347-355.

Low, Emile. "A Natural Railway Tunnel." *Engineering News and American Railway Journal,* 4 May 1893.

Marvel, William. "The Great Impostors." *The Blue and Gray Magazine,* February 1991.

McCabe, James Dabney. *The Great Republic: A Descriptive, Statistical and Historical View of the States and Territories of the American Union.* Philadelphia: W. B. Evans and Company, 1871.

McCrary, Ben C. "Early Man in Virginia." J. N. McDonald and S. O. Bird, eds. *The Quaternary of Virginia—A Symposium Volume. Virginia Division of Mineral Resources Publication* 75 (1986).

Milici, R. C. "The Geology of Natural Tunnel State Park." *Virginia Minerals* 36, no. 3 (1990).

Morris, Charles and H. G. Leigh., eds. *With the World's Greatest Travellers.* Chicago: Chicago Union Book Company, 1901.

"Mountain Scenery of Virginia." *The Southern Literary Messenger; Devoted to Every Department of Literature and the Fine Arts* 10, no. 12 (1844).

Murray, Hugh. *The Encyclopaedia of Geography Comprising a Complete Description of the Earth, Physical, Statistical, Civil, and Political; Exhibitng Its Relation to the Heavenly Bodies, Its Physical Structure, the Natural History of Each Country, and the Industry.* Philadelphia: Blanchard and Lea, 1852.

"Natural Tunnel." *Trains Magazine,* January 1944.

Pearcy, Andrew Jackson. Extracts from personal diary for 1902, used by permission of family.

Peck, H. C. and Theo Bliss, eds. *Adventures of Hunters and Travellers, and Narratives of Border Warfare. By an Old Hunter.* Philadelphia: by the authors, 1852.

Phillips, V. N. (Bud). *Bristol Tennessee/Virginia, A History—1852-1900.* Johnson City, Tenn.: The Overmountain Press, 1992.

Pollard, Edward A. *The Virginia Tourist.* Philadelphia: J. P. Lippincott and Company, 1871.

Prescott, E. J. *The Story of the Virginia Coal and Iron Company, 1882-1945.* Big Stone Gap, Va.: Virginia Coal and Iron Company, 1946.

Prince, Richard E. *Southern Railway System Steam Locomotives and Boats.* Green River, Wyo.: Richard E. Prince, 1970.

Ripley, George and Charles A. Dana, eds. *The American Cyclopaedia: A Popular Dictionary Of General Knowledge.* New York: D. Appleton and Company, 1873.

Robertson, G. Alexander. "Vanishing American." *The National Speleological Society News* 12, no. 4 (1954).

Rothwell, R. P. and R. W. Raymond, eds."The Great Natural Tunnel on the South Atlantic & Ohio Railroad, Virginia." *The Engineering and Mining Journal and Coal* 45, no. 1 (1888).

Ruffner, Rev. H., D. D. "Notes of a Tour from Va. to Tennessee, Chapter IV." *The Southern Literary Messenger* 5, no. 4 (1839).

_____. "Judith Bensaddi: A Tale, Number I." *The Southern Literary Messenger* 5, no. 7 (1839).

Scribner, Robert L. "A Natural Tunnel." *Virginia Cavalcade* V, no. 2 (1955).

Shaler, N. S. "Caverns and Cavern Life." *Scribner's Magazine* 2, no. 4 (1887).

Smith, J. Calvin. *Harper's Statistical Gazetteer of the World.* New York: Harper and Brothers, 1855.

South Atlantic and Ohio Railroad. *Over the Picturesque Route of the South Atlantic and Ohio Railroad from Bristol Va., to the Great Natural Tunnel, and Big Stone Gap.* New York: The Giles Company, 1890.

The Stranger's Guide and Official Directory for the City of Richmond. Richmond, Va.: George P. Evan & Co., 1863.

"Summer Travel in the South." *The Southern Quarterly Review* 2, no. 3 (1850).

Summers, Lewis Preston. *History of Southwest Virginia, 1746-1786, Washington County 1777-1870.* Johnson City, Tenn.: The Overmountain Press, 1989.

_____. *Annals of Southwest Virginia, 1769-1800.* Johnson City, Tenn.: The Overmountain Press, 1992.

Sweet, Palmer C. *Directory of the Mineral Industry in Virginia-1983.* Virginia Division of Mineral Resources, 1983.

Ties, The Southern Railway System Magazine 2, no. 1 (1948).

Thomas, J. and T. Baldwin, eds. *Lippincott's Pronouncing Gazetteer.* Philadelphia: J. B. Lippincott and Company, 1856.

Thornbury, William D. *Principles of Geomorphology.* New York: John Wiley and Sons, Inc., 1954.

"The Tunnel and Cave in Scott County." *The Richmond Daily Whig,* 14 September 1872.

"Virginia Scenery." *Debow's Review, Agricultural, Commercial, Industrial Progress and Resources* 10, no. 3 (1851).

Walker, Kyle M. *Horse Feathers and Frog Hair: The Life and Times of a Country Boy.* Unpublished, 1989.

Waltham, Tony. "Natural Tunnel, Virginia." *Cave Science* 15, no. 1 (1988).

Whittemore, R. E., et al. "Natural Tunnel Caverns Map." Virginia Section of the American Institute of Professional Geologists: Unpublished, 1993.

"Winter in the South." *Harper's New Monthly Magazine* 15, no. 89 (1857).

Wise County Historical Society. *The Heritage of Wise County and the City of Norton: 1856-2001.* Wise, Va.: Wise County Historical Society, 2001.

Wolfe, Ed. *The Interstate Railroad, History of an Appalachian Coal Road.* Silver Spring, Md.: Old Line Graphics, 1994.

Woodward, H. P. "Natural Bridge and Natural Tunnel, Virginia." *Journal of Geology* 44, no. 5 (1936): 604-616.

143

Online Sources

Anderson, H. Allen. "Long, Stephen Harriman," *The Handbook of Texas Online*, 4 December 2002, <http://www.tsha.utexas.edu/handbook/online/articles/view/LL/flo13.html> (accessed 27 October 2004).

Irvine, R. Tate. "Wise County in War Time: A Community History," New River Notes, 2004, <http://www.ls.net/~newriver/va/wiseww1.htm> (accessed 27 October 2004).

National Park Service. "Outline of Prehistory and History: Southeastern North America and the Caribbean," 2001, <http://www.cr.nps.gov/seac/outline/index.htm> (accessed 27 October 2004).

Wood, David L. "The Famous Explorers of Minnesota Who Have Mountains in the Colorado Rockies Named After Them Page," 27 March 1999, <http://dlwgraphics.com/Mnexplrr.htm> (accessed 27 October 2004).

Note: Many of the publications listed here, especially those of the 19th Century, can be accessed digitally through the Making of American Project, funded by the Andrew W. Mellon Foundation and a collaborative effort between the University of Michigan (http://moa.umdl.umich.edu/) and Cornell University (http://cdl.library.cornell.edu/moa/).

Index

Tony Scales was born in Bristol, Virginia, and raised in Bristol, Tennessee—and thus considers himself a true "Franklinian." He earned master's and bachelor's degrees in geology from the University of Tennessee. A Certified Professional Geologist, he has spent his professional career in the coalfields of Southwest Virginia. He has published a number of professional articles; a casual start on such a one, combined with his love of a place, grew into this, his first book. He resides in Big Stone Gap, Virginia, with his wife and son, with an "occasional" visit to Natural Tunnel.

OTHER BOOKS OF SOUTHWEST VIRGINIA INTEREST

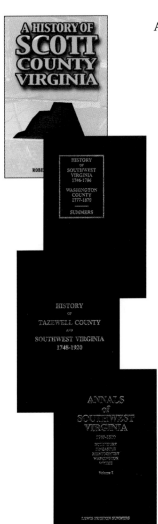

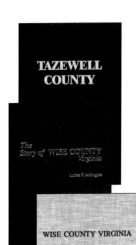

A History of Scott County, Virginia
Robert M. Addington
ISBN: 0-932807-67-4
$24.95 / Hardcover

**History of Southwest Virginia
1746-1786
Washington County 1777-1870**
Lewis Preston Summers
ISBN: 0-932807-43-7
$42.50 / Hardcover

**History of Tazewell County
and Southwest Virginia
1748-1920**
William C. Pendleton
ISBN: 0-932807-39-9
$32.50 / Hardcover

**Annals of
Southwest Virginia
1769-1800**
Lewis Preston Summers
ISBN: 0-932807-80-1
$74.95 / Hardcover
Two Volumes

Tazewell County
Louise Leslie
ISBN: 1-57072-031-2
$34.95 / Hardcover

**The Story of Wise County,
Virginia**
Charles A. Johnson
ISBN: 0-932807-30-5
$24.95 / Hardcover

Wise County, Virginia
Luther F. Addington
ISBN: 0-932807-29-1
$27.95 / Hardcover

**School and Community History of
Dickenson County, Virginia**
Edited by Dennis Reedy
ISBN: 1-57072-010-X
$21.95 / Hardcover

**The Life and Adventures of
Wilburn Waters**
Charles B. Coale
ISBN: 1-57072-003-7
$5.95 / Trade Paper

SOUTHWEST VIRGINIA CROSSROADS BY JOE TENNIS

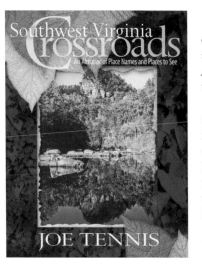

The mountains, rivers, and lakes of Southwest Virginia have invited explorers since the mid-1700s. Now this land beckons the modern traveler with its siren song of beauty, wonder, and history. *Southwest Virginia Crossroads: An Almanac of Place Names and Places to See* extols the virtues of this national treasure and serves as a guide for those who want to find the best of America.

As you journey with author Joe Tennis through *Southwest Virginia Crossroads,* he relates the history of the land and its people, chronicling the fascinating stories birthed in this fabled region, as well as age-old place-names and their origins. County maps and detailed directions lead you to all the little- and best-known attractions housed in cities and towns like Bristol and Abingdon or sheltered within the rolling farmland and weathered mountains. Even those familiar with the area will want to visit waterfalls, lakes, towns, cities, restaurants, and historical sites discovered in the pages of this comprehensive work.

Whether on the car dashboard or at home on the coffee table, *Southwest Virginia Crossroads* is a wealth of knowledge and a delight to read.

ISBN: 1-57072-256-0 / $29.95 / Trade Paper

BRISTOL HISTORY BY V. N. (BUD) PHILLIPS

Bristol Tennessee / Virginia:
A History—1852-1900
ISBN: 0-932807-63-1
$27.95 / Hardcover

The Book of Kings
ISBN: 1-57072-083-5
$29.95 / Hardcover

Between the States:
Bristol Tennessee / Virginia
During the Civil War
ISBN: 1-57072-068-1
$24.95 / Hardcover

Pioneers in Paradise
Legends and Stories from Bristol
Tennessee/Virginia
ISBN: 1-57072-234-X
$29.95 / Hardcover